THE UK AIR FRYER COOK FOR BEGINNERS

CW00468976

Effortless, Affordable & Delicious Recipes
All Using European Measurements &
UK Ingredients- Dinners, Sides, Lunch,
Breakfasts & More

By

Hannah Holmes

© **Copyright 2022 Hannah Holmes- All rights reserved.**
The content contained within this book may not be reproduced, duplicated or transmitted without
direct written permission from the author or the publisher.
Under no circumstances will any blame or legal responsibility be held against the publisher, or
author, for any damages, reparation, or monetary loss due to the information contained within this
book. Either directly or indirectly.

LEGAL NOTICE:
This book is copyright protected. This book is only for personal use. You cannot amend, distribute,
sell, use, quote or paraphrase any part, or the content within this book, without the consent of the
author or publisher.

DISCLAIMER NOTICE:
Please note the information contained within this document is for educational and entertainment
purposes only. All effort has been executed to present accurate, up to date, and reliable, complete
information. No warranties of any kind are declared or implied. Readers acknowledge that the
author is not engaging in the rendering of legal, financial, medical or professional advice.
The content within this book has been derived from various sources. By reading this document,
the reader agrees that under no circumstances is the author responsible for any losses, direct or
indirect, which are incurred as a result of the use of the information contained within this document,
including, but not limited to: errors, omissions, or inaccuracies.

Table of Contents

About The Author ... 1
INTRODUCTION ... 2
Answers to All Your Air Fryer Questions ... 3
Best and Worst Things to Make in your Air Fryer ... 5
Benefits of Air Frying ... 8
Chef's Notes ... 10

CHAPTER 1 BREAKFAST ... **11**
Breakfast Burrito ... 12
Classic Breakfast Muffins ... 12
Egg Club Sandwich ... 13
Baked Eggs in Avocado ... 13
Granola-Style Bars ... 14
Breakfast Brioche Bake with Peaches ... 14
English Breakfast ... 15
Classic Potato Rösti ... 15
Croissant Sausage Rolls ... 16
Spicy Bean Quesadillas ... 16
Omelette with Spinach and Bacon ... 17
Cheesy Asparagus Frittata ... 17
Baked Fruit Compote ... 18
Scrambled Eggs on Toast ... 18
Tuna Soufflé Tart ... 19
Tofu Sandwich ... 19
Roasted Pumpkin with Cheese ... 20
Flapjacks with Raspberry Jam ... 20
Bacon Egg Cups ... 21
Mini Breakfast Portobellas ... 21
French Toast ... 22
Halloumi Fries ... 22

CHAPTER 2 POULTRY ... **23**
Chicken Nuggets ... 24
Turkey Satay-Style Salad ... 24
Stuffed Chicken ... 25
Duck Traybake ... 25
Tandoori Chicken ... 26
Traditional Chicken Biryani ... 26
Turkey Ragù ... 27
Baked Meatballs ... 27
Spicy Turkey Meatloaf ... 28
Jerk Turkey ... 28
Chicken Salad with Baby Spinach ... 29
Easy Chicken Bake ... 29
Spicy Chicken with Cherry Tomatoes ... 30
Turkey Skewers ... 30
Buffalo Chicken Wings ... 31
Chicken Legs with Carrots ... 31
Roast Turkey ... 32
Chicken Souvlaki ... 32
Chicken with Rosemary Potatoes ... 33
Chicken Fajitas ... 33

Sichuan Duck Wings ... 34
Glazed Duck Legs ... 34

CHAPTER 3 MEAT ... **35**
Hot Spicy Meatballs ... 36
Spicy Pork Chops ... 36
Crackled Pork Belly ... 37
Glazed Pork Loin ... 37
Italian Meatloaf ... 38
Barbecued Skirt Steak ... 38
Restaurant-Style Cheeseburger ... 39
Sticky Ribs ... 39
Sausage & Pepper Pilaf ... 40
Easy Wonton Cups ... 40
Pork Hot Pot ... 41
Beef Wellington ... 41
Pork Carnitas ... 42
Roast Pork ... 42
Asian Sweet and Sour Pork ... 43
Meatball Sliders ... 43
Fall-off-the-Bone Spare Ribs ... 44
Pork Sandwiches ... 44
Steak with Cherry Tomatoes ... 45
Cheesy Pork Fillet ... 45
Pork Chops with Peppers ... 46
Pork Medallions ... 46

CHAPTER 4 FISH & SEAFOOD ... **47**
Fish and Chips ... 48
Roast Fish ... 48
Grilled Lobster Tails ... 49
Swordfish Steak ... 49
Festive Haddock Gratin ... 50
Cajun Shrimp ... 50
Tuna Niçoise Salad ... 51
Fish Fingers ... 51
Tangy Sea Scallops ... 52
Spicy Tiger Prawns ... 52
Saucy Sea Bass ... 53
Crab Croquettes ... 53
Creamy Sea Trout Salad ... 54
Ginger Garlicky Cod Fish ... 54
Scallop Salad ... 55
Tilapia Fillets with Asparagus ... 55
Calamari Rings ... 56
Fish En Papillote ... 56
Shrimp Salad ... 57
Tuna with Horseradish Sauce ... 57
Salmon Fish Cakes ... 58

CHAPTER 5 SIDE DISHES & APPETIZERS ... **59**
Herb Roast Potatoes ... 60
Courgette Fritters ... 60

Traditional Ratatouille		Easy Granola	77
Butter Cabbage		Crispy Paprika Chickpeas	77
Tofu with Vegetables		Potato and Kale Croquettes	78
Beet and Avocado Salad		Millet and Bean Burgers	78
Griddled Aubergine Rounds		BBQ Soy Curls	79
Butter Garlic Asparagus		Cauliflower Croquettes	79
Pigs-in-Blankets		"Cheese" Brussels Sprouts	80
Okra Chips		Spinach Polenta Stacks	80
Mozzarella Sticks		Vegan Gyro	81
Sweet Potato Chips		Vegan Wraps	81

61	Easy Granola
61	Crispy Paprika Chickpeas
62	Potato and Kale Croquettes
62	Millet and Bean Burgers
63	BBQ Soy Curls
63	Cauliflower Croquettes
64	"Cheese" Brussels Sprouts
64	Spinach Polenta Stacks
65	Vegan Gyro
65	Vegan Wraps

Traditional Ratatouille
Butter Cabbage
Tofu with Vegetables
Beet and Avocado Salad
Griddled Aubergine Rounds
Butter Garlic Asparagus
Pigs-in-Blankets
Okra Chips
Mozzarella Sticks
Sweet Potato Chips
Broccoli with Bacon
Spicy Stuffed Mushrooms
Roasted Vegetables
Roasted Butternut Squash Mash
Classic Potato Latkes
Corn on the Cob
Fennel with Cherry Tomatoes
Carrots with Leek and Tomatoes
Vegetarian Stuffed Peppers
Szechuan Green Beans

CHAPTER 6 VEGAN

Aubergine Burger
Stuffed Winter Squash
Tempeh Salad
Vegan Tacos
Tofu-Stuffed Mushrooms
Vegan French Toast
Stuffed Aubergine Rolls
Traditional Falafel
Cauliflower Wings
Tofu Nuggets

61   Easy Granola   77
61   Crispy Paprika Chickpeas   77
62   Potato and Kale Croquettes   78
62   Millet and Bean Burgers   78
63   BBQ Soy Curls   79
63   Cauliflower Croquettes   79
64   "Cheese" Brussels Sprouts   80
64   Spinach Polenta Stacks   80
65   Vegan Gyro   81
65   Vegan Wraps   81
66   **CHAPTER 7 DESSERTS**   **82**
66   Chocolate Chip Cookies   83
67   Easy Mince Pies   83
67   Anise Bread Pudding Cups   84
68   Chocolate Brownies   84
68   Stuffed Apples   85
69   Chocolate and Blackberry Wontons   85
69   Mug Cake   86
70   Roasted Fruit Salad   86
70   Banana Muffins   87
71   Peanut Butter Cinnamon Cookies   87
72   Chocolate Cupcakes   88
72   Mini Berry Cheesecakes   88
73   Apple Fritters   89
73   Plum Crumble   89
74   Authentic Churros   90
74   Banana Fritters   90
75   Crème Brûlée   91
75   Pear Pie Samosas   91
76   Berry Crisp   92
76   Chocolate Fudge with Almonds   92
    Apple Chips   93

About The Author

A group of Chefs trying to make British cookbooks amazing again!

We know how busy you are, that is why we aim to make our recipes as easy, budget friendly and, of course, as delicious as possible, so you can cook up meals you look forward to that nourish you simultaneously. (And anyone you're cooking for!)

With every book we create we also include a Bonus fully coloured PDF meaning each recipe has a beautiful coloured photo!

We couldn't include them in the book due to printing costs and we wanted to keep the books as affordable as possible. We hope you enjoy!

Also, if you have any feedback on how we can improve this book & further books please email us that and we will make all the changes we can. Or, if you have any issues / troubles then simply email us those and our customer support team will be happy to help.

As already mentioned we can't add the colour photos inside the book due to printing costs (the book would be unaffordable), but any other improvements we would love to make with your help!

Our customer support email is Anthonypublishing123@gmail.com – We hope to hear from you!

Happy Cooking!

INTRODUCTION

Most of with a busy lifestyle find it difficult to prepare good-quality meals at home, often opting for takeaways and microwave food that affect our health in many ways. I was in the same boat, struggling to balance my career and my healthy eating choices. I was desperately looking for a way to make my diet healthier.

I have always been in a love/hate relationship with food. For years, I would find myself reaching for fried food not only to feel better or cope with stress but also to reward myself for accomplishments. It made me frustrated. When I first saw an Air Fryer in a food magazine, I thought it seemed like a great way to fry my favourite foods, such as fish and chips, doughnuts, and burgers, in a healthy way. I didn't own a deep-fryer and microwave, so it seemed like a perfect alternative to my bulky outdoor grill and all the frying pans I already have in my kitchen. Healthy fried food that is tender inside and crispy outside and doesn't leave you with a smoky kitchen sounded really good to me!

Another reason I decided to buy my Air Fryer was that I was obese and at great risk of increased high blood pressure, high cholesterol levels, and diabetes. Weight loss is not just about aesthetic beauty; obesity can increase the risk of several serious diseases, including cardiovascular disease and certain types of cancers. Carrying extra pounds can cause hormonal disbalance as well as metabolic disorders. In light of that awareness, I wanted to cut some calories but not miss out on my favourite fried foods. Air Fryers use a scant amount of oil, so they can significantly cut the fat content of your food (up to 80%). It means that using your Air Fryer can significantly cut down your daily calorie intake. Since Air Fryers reduce all those greasy calories, this new eating habit helped me to drop some weight and improve my overall health. I thought that switching to air-fried foods may be an easy way to achieve weight loss and maintain an ideal BMI (body mass index). Plus, this was a great way to improve my long-term health as I age. Luckily for me, I was right! As an Air Fryer beginner, I started by cooking fish and chips in my Air Fryer, and I was blown away by how much it exceeded my expectations! Then I ventured into poultry, snacks, and desserts, and I soon realized that I could adapt a lot of recipes for my Air Fryer; I could grill, bake, reheat, and roast the food in my Air Fryer. Once I started using my Air Fryer, I couldn't stop – this mini oven became my go-to kitchen gadget for all my culinary dreams! This little kitchen companion did everything my large oven has ever done and more. Unlike the oven, it uses less electricity and cooks faster. With my hectic lifestyle, this means a lot to me!

I am still in love with my Air Fryer, experimenting with traditional recipes and adapting some of my fancier dishes to work with this amazing kitchen gadget. I realized there is a wide variety of recipes you can cook in Air Fryers. That is where this recipe collection comes in! This book teaches basic air frying techniques and provides beginners with all the necessary information about Air Fryers; anyone can use it for inspiration, including seasoned cooks. If you do not like processed foods, this book may become your go-to source for the best Air Fryer recipes. My recipes use common ingredients without chemicals and packaged foods. If you want to cook delicious meals without spending all day in the kitchen, this book will surprise you.

The best part? You can prepare most of the recipes in 30 minutes or less. I divided the recipes into chapters by food groups and categories of meals. There are the following chapters: breakfast, poultry, meat, fish & seafood, side dishes & appetizers, vegan, and desserts. Each recipe is accompanied by the preparation time, cooking time, number of servings it yields, the list of ingredients, and step-by-step instructions. If you try to watch what you eat, I got you covered; the recipes include complete nutrition facts (calories, protein, carbohydrates, and fat content). Therefore, read your recipe thoroughly before proceeding. Although you will find a lot of useful information in this cookbook, it is extremely important to read the manual that comes with your machine.

Aside from allowing me to cook the healthiest fried food ever, suitability and adaptability are the best features of my Air Fryer. The process is easy-to-follow: add your ingredients to the removable cooking basket, drizzle a scant amount of good quality oil, set the cooking time and temperature and then watch the magic happen as super-heated air starts circulating around your food, cooking it efficiently and evenly.

Have you ever wondered about the secret behind the most popular restaurant foods such as steaks, fish filets, Buffalo wings, or beef burgers? Would you like to be able to make the best fried foods in the comfort of your home? We are about to reveal kitchen secrets that professional chefs probably won't tell you. I am so happy with my Air Fryer, so I wanted to share my experience and tips with you to help you adopt healthy eating habits and make cooking fun and enjoyable. This is all about our fast-food favourites and classic fried foods, from cheeseburgers and chicken wings to potato chips and churros. Enjoy!

Answers to All Your Air Fryer Questions

What is an Air Fryer?

In recent years, we have seen many alternative cooking techniques, so it's not always easy to know what to choose. New appliances are intended to simplify cooking and improve your life. If you like to keep the time you spend in your kitchen to a minimum, you will be surprised by the versatility of Air Fryers. As revolutionary kitchen gadgets, Air Fryers trap the heat produced by a heating element and use a powerful fan to move hot air around the food, cooking it from all sides. With its remarkable features, this type of small convection cooker has become increasingly popular in recent years. Unlike deep fryers, pans, and grills, it comes with no smoke, splashes, and unpleasant odours. This means no more slaving over a hot stove, less mess, and less stress. I really enjoy these hands-free and odour-free cooking experiences!

How does an Air Fryer work?

Air Fryers use unique Rapid Air Technology to cook foods. In fact, this is a chemical reaction known as the Maillard effect. According to Wikipedia, "The Maillard reaction (/maɪjɑr/ my-YAR; French: [maja]) is a chemical reaction between amino acids and reducing sugars that gives browned food its distinctive flavour." There are many things you can cook in your Air Fryer. You can have the taste of the best homemade meals that used to take too long in an oven or on a stove, cooked in your new powerful machine in a matter of minutes.

Does food lose its texture and crispiness?

Speaking from my own experience, using less oil does not necessarily mean that food will lose its signature crispy deliciousness. Many studies have proven that as well. There are numerous factors that contribute to the crispiness of fried foods. For instance, the type of food is as important as the right cooking time. In order for your food to cook evenly, it's essential to cut it in the same size. When it comes to starchy foods such as potato chips, soaking is a good way to remove excess starch. Make sure to pat your soaked potatoes dry with a paper or tea towel and your Air Fryer will cook them to crispy perfection! And last but not least, do not overcrowd the cooking basket and avoid the temptation to cook more than one kind of food at a time. This is one of the Air Fryer's essential rules: foods need to be cooked in a single layer because overcrowding the basket will prevent the hot air from circulating evenly around each item. That may result in food that is not evenly brown, soggy, and uncooked. Flip your food once halfway through, just as you would if you were cooking it in an oven or on a grill. It is important to follow these rules if you want evenly cooked food with a nice, crunchy surface.

What is the best oil to use for air-frying?

Selecting an oil for air-frying with a suitable smoke point is the key challenge. In theory, Air Fryers can cook food with no oil at all. But, if you prepare raw food without oil, it can stick to the bottom of the cooking basket and become tasteless due to high temperature and hot air circulation. Therefore, make sure to spray the food and the cooking basket with a thin layer of oil. That brings us to our next important point – the smoking point. Nutritionists recommend using oils with a smoke point of 200 degrees C and higher, so choose your oil wisely. The higher the smoke point, the better; plus, make sure to use unrefined monounsaturated and polyunsaturated fats. The best options are olive oil, avocado oil, and peanut oil, as the temperature in an Air Fryer reaches 200 degrees C. According to the Acta Scientific Nutritional Health study, the olive oil's smoke point does not matter since it has great oxidative stability, producing lower levels of trans fats and other harmful bioproducts; compared to other oils that have a higher smoke point, EVOO is an excellent option for air frying.

Can I use an Air Fryer for different cooking techniques?

Once you understand how Air Fryer works, you will use it to cook fresh and frozen food, including meat, seafood, fruits, and vegetables. Let's take a closer look at the Air Fryer's functions.

If you want to grill the food in your Air Fryer, it is important to select a high temperature and short cooking time. You do not have to turn the ingredients; all you have to do is to shake the cooking basket halfway through the cooking time. Many Air Fryers come with a grill pan. When it comes to baking, you can use baking tins, muffin tins and silicone moulds to prepare baked goods and desserts. You can also broil your food to enhance the quality and flavour of your favourite meals, such as casseroles and meat dishes.

With your Air Fryer, you can roast vegetables and meat, just like you would in the oven. Plus, Air Fryers can toast your food faster than a regular oven. When placing food in the cooking basket, you can add parchment liners to make the cleaning process easier. You can use your Air Fryer to reheat leftovers and make them taste freshly-cooked and delicious again. To warm or reheat your food, set your machine at 150°C for up to 10 minutes.

Frying is, as the name implies, one of the essential functions of Air Fryers; that is the main reason why people decide to buy an Air Fryer. Splattering oil and messy clean-up will become a thing of the past for you! Air Fryers cook meals such as potato chips, mozzarella sticks, chicken wings, and calamari to a golden perfection over and over again. And most importantly, they are crispy and delicious without the extra calories.

Do I need to preheat my Air Fryer?

The short answer is no, you do not need to preheat your Air Fryer, but it is recommended. You can quickly preheat the machine for 2 minutes before adding the food to the cooking basket. You can skip that step if you are planning to fry, reheat, or toast your food, but it's best to preheat it if you want to bake and roast the food. As for frozen foods such as nuggets and fish, they will benefit from preheating.

How should I bread food for an Air Fryer?

Breading is a crucial part of many Air Fryer recipes. It is important to use the right amount of ingredients so your breading will not fall off and make a mess. There are three steps to follow: coat foods with flour first, then dip in egg and roll them over the crumbs, pressing firmly to coat them on all sides. A pro-tip: chilling the breaded foods in your fridge for about 30 minutes before air-frying will give the coating more time to stick to the food and that can help it stay in place in the Air Fryer. Finally, drizzle your food with cooking spray. It will not only help cook the food evenly, but also prevent your food from drying out, contributing to a crispy, moist, and delicious coating.

What accessories do I need for my Air Fryer?

It all depends on what you want to cook in your Air Fryer. For instance, if you love grilling, a grill plate and silicone tongs are a must. If you love baking breads and muffins, baking tins and silicone moulds will fulfil your culinary dreams. Whatever you do, make sure to use heat proof accessories that fit inside the cooking basket properly. Useful Air Fryer accessories include skewers on double layer rack, baking tins, cupcake cases, silicone tart and pie moulds, grill pans, souffle dishes, silicone mat, pizza pan, pastry brush, silicone double spatula, cake tins, and so on.

Best and Worst Things to Make in your Air Fryer

Chicken

Lean cuts of poultry, such as boneless turkey breasts, boneless chicken breasts, or turkey mince with little or no fat content, require oil to brown and crisp up. Therefore, brush boneless chicken breasts, tenders, nuggets, fillets, and chicken meatballs with non-stick cooking oil before adding them to the Air Fryer cooking basket. When it comes to the cooking time and temperature, it is important to read the manufacturer's instructions; however, for safe consumption, use a food thermometer to check the internal temperature of meat. Be sure to pat the chicken dry with paper towels before putting it in the cooking basket to achieve crisp perfection.

I included Air Fryer cooking charts for each food group, but please note that some values may be rounded. Remember that cooking time may vary depending on your food's size, thickness, etc. Always check the food before eating, and if it's not done, set the timer for a few extra minutes; repeat the process until you are happy with the result. The recommended safe minimum internal temperatures for cooked poultry are as follows: 75°C for chicken, 70°C for turkey, and 52°C for duck.

CHICKEN (400-600g)	Temperature	Time (minutes)		Temperature	Time (minutes)
Breasts, bone-in	180°C	20-22	Tenders	180°C	8-10
Drumettes, bone-in	190°C	20-22	Thighs, bone-in	180°C	20-22
Legs, boneless	180°C	20-22	Thigs	180°C	18-20
Legs, bone-in	180°C	28-30	Whole chicken	180°C	70-750
Nuggets	200°C	9-10	Wings	180°C	15-20

Pork and Beef

Pork and beef ribs do not require any added oil due to their natural fat content. They are already tender and juicy, so just coat them with dry seasoning to achieve crispier results. You can marinate the meat, especially if you tend to use lean cuts. While the meat is cooking in your Air Fryer, you can also add your marinade or sauce of choice. Basting and mop sauces will add a special flavour to your favourite cut of meat. When it comes to basting with the leftover marinade, there is the risk of cross-contamination, i.e., adding back the bacteria from the raw meat to the prepared meal. To avoid the risk, keep in mind that the last application must be at least 10 minutes before the end of the cooking time. You can also use spraying to tenderize meat and help it retain moisture; so, grab a spray bottle and spritz the meat with a very thin mixture of lemon juice or vinegar.

How do you determine if meat is cooked properly? Insert an instant-read (or meat) thermometer through the side into the thickest part of the meat without touching the bones. The recommended safe minimum internal temperatures for cooked beef are as follows: 65-70°C for medium, 70°C for medium well-done, and 75°C for well-done. The recommended safe minimum internal temperatures for cooked pork are as follows: 68°C for chops, ribs, and roast; 71°C for pork mince and 63°C for tenderloin.

PORK (400-600g)	Temperature	Time (minutes)		Temperature	Time (minutes)
Bacon, thin-cut	200°C	5-7	Shoulder	200°C	25
Bacon, thick-cut	200°C	6-10	Shoulder	200°C	13-15
Belly	160°C	50-55	Shoulder	200°C	25-35
Loin	180°C	50-55	Steak	200°C	10-12
Chops	190°C	10-15	Tenderloin	200°C	20-22

BEEF (400-600g)	Temperature	Time (minutes)		Temperature	Time (minutes)
Burger	180°C	15-16	Meatballs, big	180°C	10-10
Filet mignon	180°C	18-19	Ribeye	200°C	10-15
Flank steak	180°C	15-18	Round roast	200°C	45-55
London broil	180°C	20-28	Ribs	200°C	30-35
Meatballs, small	180°C	9-10	Sirloin Steak	200°C	10-15

Fish & Seafood

Seafood, such as boneless fish fillets and shrimp, also need to be tossed in a tiny amount of oil before air frying. Food experts recommend sprinkling them with seasoning mix before air frying, and they will pack a lot of flavour. The recommended safe minimum internal temperature for cooked fish is 63°C and for crustaceans is 62°C. Cooking seafood this way not only makes it flavourful and tender but, thanks to the short cooking times and powerful hot air, it will also preserve the nutrients and vitamins. Fish is an excellent source of omega-3 fatty acids, vitamin D, vitamin B2, calcium, and phosphorus. Health experts recommend eating fish at least two times a week.

SEAFOOD (400-600g)	Temperature	Time (minutes)		Temperature	Time (minutes)
Calamari	200°C	4-5	Scallops	200°C	6-7
Crab cakes	200°C	10-11	Sea bass	190°C	12-13
Fish sticks	200°C	6-10	Shrimp	200°C	5-6
White fish fillet	200°C	10-12	Swordfish	200°C	10-12
Salmon fillet	180°C	12	Tuna	200°C	12-13

Vegetables

Oh, veggies! I just love them! There are many recipes for beginner cooks to make in an Air Fryer – anything from potato mash to roasted and grilled vegetables! Plus, an Air Fryer allows you to use up any inexpensive and boring vegetables, which would otherwise end up in a rubbish bin. I hope you will find your favourite recipes for vegetable dishes in this collection.

Vegetables are one of the quickest items to prepare in an Air Fryer. While retaining their valuable nutrients, you will be able to cook vegan dishes, sides, and appetizers effortlessly. A wide variety of vegetables can be cooked in your Air Fryer – butternut squash, cauliflower florets, green beans, and peppers take a little time to cook, but they come out so crispy, so delicious! From delicate greens to root vegetables, you will discover a brand-new way of enjoying vegetables. The key to the best Air Fryer vegetables is the seasoning. A good rule of thumb is to taste your veggies after cooking and adjust the seasoning!

VEGETABLES (400-600g)	Temperature	Time (minutes)		Temperature	Time (minutes)
Asparagus	200°C	5-7	Green beans	200°C	5-7
Aubergine	200°C	15	Kale	120°C	12
Broccoli	200°C	6	Mushrooms	200°C	5
Brussels Sprouts	180°C	15	Parsnips	180°C	15
Carrots	180°C	13-15	Peppers	200°C	15
Cauliflower	200°C	12-15	Potatoes	200°C	15
Fennel, sliced	180°C	15	Tomato, slices	180°C	10

Besides being super useful for cooking meat and vegetables, your Air Fryer can also cook delectable desserts! A moist and crunchy fruit crumble, rustic baked fruit compote, old-fashioned Crème Brulé, and fudgy brownies that taste and look like they came from a 5-star restaurant! Best of all, no one will know it only took you 10 to 15 minutes to create it! This brings us to the next point: What should not you cook in Air Fryers? Food with a wet batter and grilled cheese are not suitable for Air Fryers, because wet coating and melting cheese will just drip off while the food cooks. You should not cook leafy greens because they are too delicate and lightweight for high temperatures and powerful Air Fryer fans. An exception to this tule would be the kale chips recipe; you can cook kale chips at 120°C for approximately 12 minutes, shaking the basket periodically to ensure even browning. It goes without saying that you cannot cook soups and stews, as well as any liquid foods.

Benefits of Air Frying

Health benefits

Have you ever wondered how bad junk food and re-used oils are for our health? Simple carbohydrates in highly processed food and refined sugars may predispose you to chronic disease. Processed red meat can increase cancer risk through compounds like heterocyclic amines. Cooking carbohydrate-rich foods in hot oil can create potentially dangerous compounds such as acrylamide that is possibly carcinogenic to humans; many studies have found a link between acrylamide and an increased risk of ovarian and kidney cancers. And so on, and so on. Air-frying may help lower the formation of many harmful compounds, but, undoubtedly, further research is needed to provide definitive results. Moreover, many studies have proven that a higher intake of fat has been associated with an increased risk of serious conditions such as inflammation, cardiovascular disease, and atherosclerosis. Instead of submerging your food in oil, Air Fryers require just a teaspoon or two to achieve a similar crispy texture. Eliminating greasy foods is certainly essential, but we should be concerned about the food supply and chemicals. We want healthy homemade meals, not unhealthy pre-packaged foods and overprocessed ingredients. In keeping with the latest health trends of clean eating, I prefer locally grown produce and fresh, seasonal foods whenever possible. No matter how much we love to cook from scratch, spending hours in the kitchen is not realistic for most of us. Sometimes my belly cries out for comfort food, and I also have a sweet tooth. If you also like your little guilty pleasures such as snacks and sweets that make you feel good, do not worry. I personally aim to strive for progress rather than perfection. Homemade meals are much healthier because you can control what goes into your food. You can avoid GMOs, preservatives, and additives, and in general, you can limit the amounts you eat. Plus, your food is air-fried or baked; there's still room for improvement, but it is a huge step towards better health and happier life.

The bottom line is that air frying requires a tiny amount of oil, which is the key to the reduced risk of chronic disease, obesity, and even premature death.

How you can lose weight by using an Air Fryer

If you love munching crunchy bites, but do not love all those calories and fat, your Air Fryer can turn your greasy comfort food into healthier alternatives. As you probably already know, a higher intake of fried, pre-packaged food is associated with a greater risk of obesity. On the other hand, fried foods taste so good, so it is difficult to resist a junk food craving. It is wise to be aware of your eating habits and triggers for overeating unhealthy fried food. After all, balance, not calories or fat, is the key to a healthy weight; having a chocolate cake occasionally, on your birthday or celebration party, is not the same as eating doughnuts every day. Here is good news for you: there is no need to give up your favourite fried foods; consider changing the cooking method. If you want to trim your waistline, simply swap your deep-fried foods for air-fried foods.

The calories and fat content of your food are the keys to weight management. In fact, many recipes for deep-fried foods call for up to 750ml of oil; what's worse, deep fryers use cheap and re-used oil due to the cost-effectiveness. On the other hand, Air Fryer recipes call for 1 teaspoon to 1 tablespoon of a good-quality oil. It is 50 times less oil than deep fryers require! Manufacturers claim that using Air Fryers can reduce the fat content of fried foods by up to 70%. Did you know that fat contains over twice as many calories per gram as protein or carbohydrates? This can have a major impact on your weight.

Time, cost, and space-saving device

When it comes to cost-effectiveness, air fryers are more effective than utilizing an oven. Your Air Fryer can replace a lot of kitchen tools such as frying pans, toasted oven, microwave, and grills. It is a good space-saver idea, which is one of the essential reasons why people invent this amazing kitchen appliance. You can easily change the insert or remove the baking sheets to air fry and vice versa. Once you get the hang of it, you can experiment with this incredible machine and try to use it for advanced cooking techniques such as dehydrating. For instance, you can prepare dried foods, banana chips, veggie chips, sun-dried tomatoes, apple chips, curated meats, beef jerky. and much more.

Plus, there are many versions of Air Fryers, so you can choose your device based on the size of your household. Air Fryers will not take up a lot of space on the kitchen counter; they perfectly fit in a workplace break space! Air Fryers make cleaning up a cinch; food will not adhere to the non-stick surface, so you can effortlessly remove it from the Air Fryer basket using a wooden or silicone spatula.

Adaptability

Suitability and adaptability are one of the most important aspects of an Air Fryer. Besides being useful for frying, your Air Fryer can also bake, broil, roast, grill, and stir-fry. It's amazing that a single machine can perform many tasks in multiple ways! There are Air Fryers that have specific functions for different types of food. So glam! It can literarily cook the most complicated meals at the touch of a button. You can use it to prepare amazing wraps, and vegetable dishes or use a basket divider to cook several meals at the same time. Before cooking multiple items, ensure that they require the same cooking temperature. Since you can cook from frozen, use your Air Fryer to meal prep and revive your leftovers at the touch of a button.

An Air Fryer is the perfect kitchen companion for beginners because it allows you to open the drawer to check the cooking process at any time; this will not interrupt the timing of your Air Fryer, since it does not lose internal temperature. Thanks to its small cooking chamber, it does not take much time to reheat your food and continue the cooking process. Air Fryers are very simple machines, so that every beginner home cook can use them without much hassle. Whether you're a beginner or ready to expand your culinary horizons, I am so happy to welcome you into the Air Fryer world. Are you ready to discover the wonderful world of healthy homemade fried foods?

Chef's Notes

Nutrition information is calculated using an ingredient database and should be considered an estimate. Optional ingredients are not included.
Please note that some values may be rounded.

CHAPTER 1
BREAKFAST

Hello! Please scan the QR code below to access your promised bonus of all our recipes with full colored photos & beautiful designs!

It is the best we could do to keep the book as cheap as possible while providing the best value!

Also, once downloaded you can take the PDF with you digitally wherever you go- meaning you can cook these recipes wherever an Air Fryer is present!'

STEP BY STEP Guide To Access-

1. Open Your Phones (Or Any Device You Want The Book On) Back Camera. The Back Camera Is The One You use as if you are taking a picture of someone.
2. Simply point your Camera at the QR code and 'tap' the QR code with your finger to focus the camera.
3. A link / pop up will appear. Simply tap that (and make sure you have internet connection) and the FREE PDF containing all of the colored images should appear.
4. If You Click On The File And It Says 'The File Is Too Big To Preview' Simply click 'Download' and it will download the full book onto your phone!
5. Now you have access to these FOREVER. Simply 'Bookmark' The tab it opened on, or download the document and take wherever you want.
6. Repeat this on any device you want it on!

Any Issues / Feedback/ Troubleshooting please email: anthonypublishing123@gmail.com and our customer service team will help you! We want to make sure you have the BEST experience with our books!

Breakfast Burrito

How do you like your eggs? Set the timer to 5 minutes for a nice runny egg yolk. Cook the eggs longer for firm yolks, if desired.

Preparation Time	Cooking Time	Servings
	✕	🍽
10 min	6 min	2

Nutritional Information Per Serving

Energy value: 315 Kcal, Protein: 11.4g,
Carbohydrates: 31.4, Fats: 16.6

Ingredients

- 1 tsp. olive oil
- 2 eggs
- 2 whole-meal tortilla wraps
- ½ small avocado, halved
- 50g baby spinach
- 1 small ripe tomato, sliced (or ketchup)

Instructions

1. Spray tartlet moulds with olive oil. Then, crack an egg in each tartlet mould.
2. Air fry the eggs at 190°C/375°F for 4 to 5 minutes, until set. After that, warm up your tortillas at 175°C/350°F for approximately 15 seconds, until thoroughly warmed.
3. Place the avocado halves on a cutting board; now, whack the pit with the sharp end of the knife to remove it easily. Slice your avocado.
4. To assemble your burritos, divide fried eggs, avocado slices, spinach, and tomato between tortilla wraps; wrap them up and serve immediately.
5. Enjoy!

Classic Breakfast Muffins

Treat your family to this decadent breakfast muffins. Other great add-ins include sunflower seeds, raisins, and chopped almonds.

Preparation Time	Cooking Time	Servings
	✕	🍽
10 min	20 min	4

Nutritional Information Per Serving

Energy value: 205 Kcal, Protein: 6.6g,
Carbohydrates: 25.9, Fats: 8.8

Ingredients

- 1 large egg
- 50g apple sauce
- 50ml coconut yoghurt, unsweetened
- 20ml coconut oil, room temperature
- 2 tbsp. agave syrup
- 20g old-fashioned rolled oat
- 70g wholemeal flour
- 1 tbsp flaxseed meal
- 1 tsp. baking powder
- A pinch of salt
- ¼ tsp. ground cinnamon
- ¼ tsp. ground cloves
- 1 tbsp. raw pepitas (pumpkin seeds)

Instructions

1. Start by preheating your Air Fryer to 175°C/350°F. Brush a muffin tin (with 4 muffin cases) with non-stick cooking oil.
2. In a large mixing bowl, beat the egg until pale and frothy; gradually and carefully pour in the other liquid ingredients. Gradually, stir in the dry ingredients (in the order listed above). Stir with a wire whisk until a smooth batter forms. (Do not overmix your batter).
3. Afterwards, fold in your pepitas and gently stir to combine. Spoon the batter into the prepared muffin tin.
4. Cook the breakfast muffins for approximately 20 minutes. Leave them to cool completely before unmoulding and serving.
5. Bon appétit!

Egg Club Sandwich

If you like crispy sandwiches, lightly toast your bread in the preheated Air Fryer at 160°C/320°F for approximately 5 minutes. Garnish with Romaine lettuce, cress, or crisps. It's so good!

Preparation Time 10 min   **Cooking Time** 20 min   **Servings** 3

Nutritional Information Per Serving

Energy value: 325 Kcal, Protein: 13.9g, Carbohydrates: 14.9, Fats: 22.8

Ingredients

- 6 medium eggs
- Sea salt and ground black pepper, to taste
- 3 tsp. Dijon mustard
- 30g cream cheese, chopped
- 3 tbsp. mayonnaise, regular
- 3 small cornichons, thinly sliced
- 6 thick-cut slices white bread, crustless (if desired)

Instructions

1. Add the wire rack to the Air Fryer cooking basket; carefully arrange the eggs on the rack.
2. Air fry the eggs at 130°C/270°F for 15 minutes, until set. After that, lower the eggs into an ice-cold water bath (it will stop the cooking process immediately). Once the eggs are chilled, chop them with a fork and transfer the chopped eggs to a mixing bowl. Season the eggs with salt and pepper to your liking.
3. Thoroughly combine the eggs with the mustard, cheese, mayonnaise, and cornichons; Assemble three sandwiches: Place three slices of bread on a platter. Divide the egg mixture between bread slices; top with the remaining slices of bread.
4. Bake your sandwiches at 160°C/320°F for 5 minutes. Cut sandwiches into quarters, and secure them with sticks.
5. Devour!

Baked Eggs in Avocado

The recipe calls for mango chutney, but you can use any of your favourite toppings. You can double or triple the recipe ingredients to taste.

Preparation Time 10 min   **Cooking Time** 5 min   **Servings** 2

Nutritional Information Per Serving

Energy value: 510 Kcal, Protein: 15.5g, Carbohydrates: 57.4, Fats: 25.8

Ingredients

- 1 medium avocado, halved pitted, and unpeeled
- 1 tsp. olive oil
- 2 small eggs
- Sea salt and ground black pepper, to taste
- 2 small naan breads, plain
- 1 tbsp. mango chutney
-

Instructions

1. Spray avocado halves with olive oil. Carefully spoon egg yolks into the avocado holes. Then, spoon egg whites into the holes.
2. Air fry your avocado with eggs at 190°C/375°F for 4 to 5 minutes, until set. Sprinkle your egg with salt and black pepper.
3. After that, warm up your naan at 175°C/350°F for approximately 15 seconds, until thoroughly warmed.
4. Serve baked eggs in avocado halves with warmed naan and mango chutney on the side. Enjoy!

Granola-Style Bars

If you like granola for breakfast, you will love these granola-style bars. They are healthy, nutritious, and fun to make in the Air Fryer. If you do not like hemp seeds, you can add pumpkin seeds, chia seeds, or flaxseed meal.

Preparation Time 10 min

Cooking Time 20 min

Servings 3

Nutritional Information Per Serving

Energy value: 315 Kcal, Protein: 7.6g,
Carbohydrates: 32.3g, Fats: 19.3g

Ingredients

- 50g oats
- 20g coconut oil
- 30g raw pumpkin seeds, chopped
- 1 tbsp. hemp seeds, hulled (optional)
- 1 tbsp. sesame seeds
- 2 tbsp. walnuts, roughly chopped
- 50g maple syrup
- 2 dried apricots, chopped
- ¼ tsp. ground cloves
- ½ tsp. ground cinnamon

Instructions

1. In a mixing bowl, thoroughly combine all the ingredients.
2. Scrape the batter into a parchment-lined baking tray, pressing down lightly with a silicone spatula.
3. Bake your bars in the preheated Air Fryer at 180°C/360°F for approximately 20 minutes.
4. Let it cool on a wire rack and then cut it into bars.
5. Bon appétit!

Breakfast Brioche Bake with Peaches

Are you looking for a recipe for a fancy Air Fryer breakfast? This recipe will fit the bill! You can dust the brioche bake with icing sugar for an elegant presentation.

Preparation Time 10 min + soaking

Cooking Time 22 min

Servings 4

Nutritional Information Per Serving

Energy value: 325 Kcal, Protein: 11.4g,
Carbohydrates: 41.4g, Fats:13.7g

Ingredients

- 2medium eggs
- 100ml plain milk
- 100ml double cream
- 1 tbsp. honey
- ½ tsp. vanilla extract
- ¼ tsp. ground cinnamon
- 100g peach, peeled, pitted, and sliced
- 6 brioche rolls, torn into small bite-sized pieces
- 30g raw pumpkin seeds (pepitas)

Instructions

1. In a mixing bowl, whisk the eggs, milk, cream, honey, vanilla, and cinnamon until frothy.
2. Place the pieces of brioche rolls in a deep, lightly-greased baking tin; pour the egg/milk mixture over the bread layer and press with a spatula to soak well.
3. Top with peach slices and let it sit for a couple of hours.
4. Cook the brioche bake at 180°C/360°F for about 20 minutes. Scatter raw pumpkin seeds over the top and continue to bake for 2 minutes more.
5. Bon appétit!

English Breakfast

Frying is the most common method to prepare a full English breakfast, also known as a 'fry-up'. So, your Air Fryer is the perfect kitchen tool for the full English breakfast with a modern twist. You can substitute chipolatas with Lincolnshire sausage and Cumberland sausage.

Preparation Time	Cooking Time	Servings
10 min	27 min	3

Nutritional Information Per Serving
Energy value: 416 Kcal, Protein: 19.1g,
Carbohydrates: 19.1g, Fats: 29.3

Ingredients
- 3 pork chipolatas
- 3 smoked bacon rashers
- 100g brown mushrooms
- 1 small tomato, sliced
- 4 eggs
- Sea salt and ground black pepper, to taste
- ¼ tsp. red pepper flakes, crushed
- 3 large bread slices

Instructions
1. Gather all ingredients. Add sausages to the Air Fryer cooking basket and cook them at 200°C/395°F for about 10 minutes, shaking the basket halfway through the cooking time; reserve.
2. Cook the bacon slice, mushrooms, and tomatoes at 200°C/400°F for 6 to 7 minutes.
3. Season the eggs with salt, black pepper, and red pepper. Spray tartlet moulds with non-stick cooking oil. Then, crack an egg in each tartlet mould and cook them at 190°C/375°F for 4 to 5 minutes, until set.
4. Toast the slices of bread at 200°C/400°F for approximately 5 minutes.
5. Place all ingredients on serving plates and serve with reheated canned beans.
6. Bon appétit!

Classic Potato Rösti

Rösti is a traditional Swiss dish, a type of potato cake, that can be served as breakfast or a side dish. You can use King Edward, Maris Piper, or other types of floury potatoes.

Preparation Time	Cooking Time	Servings
5 min	25 min	3

Nutritional Information Per Serving
Energy value: 426 Kcal, Protein: 13.1g,
Carbohydrates: 66.6g, Fats: 12.7g

Ingredients
- 3 large potatoes, peeled
- 1 spring onion, chopped
- 1 small egg, beaten
- Sea salt and ground black pepper, to taste
- ¼ tsp. cayenne pepper
- 3 tbsp. bacon lardons

Instructions
1. Grate your potatoes and then, wring out as much liquid from them as you can, using tea towels or a cheesecloth.
2. Thoroughly combine the potatoes, with the remaining ingredients.
3. Brush the bottom of the Air Fryer cooking basket with non-stick cooking oil.
4. Divide the mixture into 3 röstis and press them slightly using a spatula.
5. Bake your röstis at 195°C/395°F for about 13 minutes. Turn them over and cook for a further 12 minutes, until thoroughly cooked.
6. Bon appétit!

Croissant Sausage Rolls

Spread your breakfast sausage meat and red onion chutney onto crescent rolls and enjoy your favourite baked goods in the comfort of your home! An onion-based chutney adds outstanding and sophisticated taste and texture to these sausage rolls.

Preparation Time	Cooking Time	Servings
10 min	10 min	3

Nutritional Information Per Serving
Energy value: 256 Kcal, Protein: 10.1g,
Carbohydrates: 28.6g, Fats: 10.5g

Ingredients
- ½ (350g) package croissant dough
- 100g breakfast sausages, casing removed
- 1 tbsp. red onion chutney
- 1 small beaten egg
- 1 tbsp. water

Instructions
1. Roll out the croissant dough and use a knife to separate the triangles. Mix the sausage meat with red onion chutney until well combined.
2. Place the sausage mixture on half of the rolls, making sure to leave ½-inch from the edges.
3. Next, roll the dough to form crescents; pinch to seal the edges. To make an egg wash, beat the egg with water.
4. Glaze the rolls with the egg wash and bake them at 185°C/365°F for 10 minutes.
5. Serve warm and enjoy!

Spicy Bean Quesadillas

This recipe may become your go-to for an easy and delicious breakfast. Filled with refried beans, Mexican cheese, and spicy tomato salsa, these quesadillas are sure to please!

Preparation Time	Cooking Time	Servings
5 min	7 min	2

Nutritional Information Per Serving
Energy value: 368 Kcal, Protein: 18.1g,
Carbohydrates: 46g, Fats: 12.5g

Ingredients
- 2 flour tortillas
- 200g refried beans, drained and warmed
- 50g Mexican cheese blend, shredded
- 20ml fresh tomato salsa
- 1 tsp. olive oil

Instructions
1. Begin by preheating your Air Fryer to 180°C/360°F.
2. Spread refried beans and cheese over one tortilla; spoon tomato salsa over the bean and cheese layer. Top with another tortilla. Place your quesadilla in the lightly-greased cooking basket and brush it with ½ teaspoon of olive oil.
3. Cook your quesadilla for about 4 minutes; flip it, brush with the remaining ½ teaspoon of olive oil, and cook on the other side for 3 minutes more. Cut into wedges (or halves) and serve hot.

Omelette with Spinach and Bacon

English mustard is the perfect ingredient to add to your omelette! English mustard consists of yellow and brown mustard seeds, but feel free to use any type of spicy mustard you have on hand. You can also use Dijon or wholegrain mustard.

Preparation Time	Cooking Time	Servings
5 min	7 min	2

Nutritional Information Per Serving

Energy value: 233 Kcal, Protein: 9.8g,
Carbohydrates: 4.4g, Fats: 19.5g

Ingredients

- 1 tsp. olive oil
- 3 large eggs
- 50g cream cheese
- ¼ tsp. ground cumin
- ½ tsp. English mustard
- 2 rashers (20g) bacon, chopped
- 1 large handful baby spinach, rinsed and torn into smaller pieces
- Sea salt and ground black pepper, to taste

Instructions

1. Brush the sides and bottom of two ramekins with olive oil. Beat the eggs in a mixing bowl, add cream cheese, ground cumin, and mustard; whisk to combine well.
2. Fold in the bacon and spinach. Divide the mixture between the prepared ramekins. Afterwards, sprinkle with salt and pepper and transfer to the Air Fryer cooking basket.
3. Bake them at 180°C/360°F for approximately 15 minutes, until a tester (fork or wooden stick) comes out dry and clean.
4. Bon appétit!

Cheesy Asparagus Frittata

How about outstanding baked eggs with crispy asparagus and mellowly cheddar cheese? A favourite European breakfast gets a makeover with this easy-to-follow Air Fryer recipe. You'll want to eat it daily!

Preparation Time	Cooking Time	Servings
5 min	8 min	3

Nutritional Information Per Serving

Energy value: 236 Kcal, Protein: 17.7g,
Carbohydrates: 4g, Fats: 16.6g

Ingredients

- 1 tsp. olive oil
- 6 large eggs
- 2 tbsp. full-fat milk
- 40g cheddar cheese, grated
- ½ tsp. cayenne pepper
- Sea salt and ground black pepper, to taste
- 8 asparagus tips, steamed

Instructions

1. Brush the sides and bottom of a tart tin with olive oil. Beat the eggs in a mixing bowl, and then, add the milk, cheese, and spices; whisk to combine well.
2. Fold in the asparagus tips and gently stir to combine. Scrape the mixture into the prepared tart tin.
3. Bake your frittata at 185°C/365°F for approximately 8 minutes, until thoroughly cooked.
4. Bon appétit!

Baked Fruit Compote

You can substitute orange juice with dessert wine and use your favourite spices like anise, vanilla bean, or nutmeg. You can eat baked fruit compote with pancakes, French toast, or porridge.

Preparation Time	Cooking Time	Servings
5 min	15 min	4

Nutritional Information Per Serving

Energy value: 266 Kcal, Protein: 2.4g,
Carbohydrates: 61.4g, Fats: 3.9g

Ingredients

- 1 medium apple, cored and diced
- 1 medium pear, cored and diced
- 100g dried prunes
- 100g dried apricots
- 1 tbsp. coconut oil
- 150ml fresh orange juice
- ½ cinnamon stick
- 4 cloves

Instructions

1. In a baking tin, toss the fruits with the remaining ingredients. Lower the baking tin into the Air Fryer cooking basket.
2. Cook the fruits in the preheated Air Fryer at 160°C/330°F for 15 minutes, stirring the compote once or twice during the cooking time.
3. Serve cold or at room temperature.
4. Devour!

Scrambled Eggs on Toast

Making air-fried scrambled eggs on toast is a great way to start your day. Perfect scrambled eggs should be fully cooked but still soft. Garnish with tomatoes, bell peppers, or air-fried sausages.

Preparation Time	Cooking Time	Servings
5 min	20 min	3

Nutritional Information Per Serving

Energy value: 222 Kcal, Protein: 14.4g,
Carbohydrates: 14.4g, Fats: 11.5g

Ingredients

- 6 medium eggs
- Sea salt and ground black pepper, to taste
- 2 tsp. butter, melted
- 3 regular slices granary bread

Instructions

1. In a mixing bowl, whisk the eggs until pale and frothy. Add the salt, pepper, and 1 teaspoon of butter, and stir to combine well.
2. Pour the egg mixture into a lightly-greased baking tray.
3. Cook scrambled eggs in the preheated Air Fryer at 190°C/370°F for about 15 minutes, or to your desired level of doneness. (Make sure to stir the eggs once or twice during the cooking time).
4. Butter your bread with the remaining 1 teaspoon of butter. Toast the slices of granary bread at 200°C/400°F for approximately 5 minutes, until golden brown.
5. Serve scrambled eggs with toast and enjoy!

Tuna Soufflé Tart

With its flavourful and delicate flesh, tuna is the perfect addition to this Air Fryer tart. You can also use smoked salmon for this recipe as well as your favourite mix-ins such as chilli pepper, chopped mushrooms, or jarred peppers. The possibilities are endless!

Preparation Time	Cooking Time	Servings
5 min	**15 min**	**4**

Nutritional Information Per Serving

Energy value: 33 Kcal, Protein: 29g,
Carbohydrates: 2g, Fats: 19.1g

Ingredients

- 1 tsp. olive oil
- 8 large eggs
- 2 tbsp. double cream
- 1 can (170g) flaked light tuna, drained
- 1 spring onion, chopped
- 60g cream cheese, room temperature
- ½ tsp. garlic granules
- Sea salt and ground black pepper, to taste

Instructions

1. Brush the sides and bottom of a soufflé dish with olive oil. Beat the eggs until pale and frothy; then, add in the double cream and mix to combine. After that, add the remaining ingredients and gently stir to combine.
2. Spoon the mixture into the prepared soufflé dish, and smooth the top with a large spatula.
3. Bake your tart at 180°C/360°F for approximately 15 minutes, until a toothpick comes out dry and clean.
4. Bon appétit!

Tofu Sandwich

Make a perfect grilled tofu sandwich in your Air Fryer! This is the basic recipe for a basic go-to breakfast sandwich, so feel free to add your favourite fillings and come up with your unique creations!

Preparation Time	Cooking Time	Servings
35 min	**15 min**	**4**

Nutritional Information Per Serving

Energy value: 190 Kcal, Protein: 7.2g,
Carbohydrates: 21.9g, Fats: 8.4g

Ingredients

- 200g block tofu
- 2 tbsp. mayonnaise
- Ground black pepper, to taste
- ½ tsp. garlic granules
- 1 tsp. smoked paprika
- 1 cup Romaine lettuce
- 8 thin bread slices

Instructions

1. Start by pressing your tofu. Place a few folded paper towels on a working surface (preferably a wooden board). Lay the block of tofu on the paper towels. Top the tofu with another layer of paper towels. Press it down with a heavy pan or pot (you can fill it with water). Allow your tofu to stand there for at least 30 minutes.
2. Cut your tofu into 8 slices and toss them with mayonnaise, black pepper, garlic, and paprika.
3. Cook your tofu in the preheated Air Fryer at 200°C/395°F for 15 minutes, until cooked through.
4. Assemble 4 sandwiches with bread slices, your air-fried tofu, and lettuce. Serve and enjoy!

Roasted Pumpkin with Cheese

This is the perfect autumn breakfast – light, tasty, and cosy. Pumpkin pairs perfectly with Ricotta cheese, but you can use any type of whey cheese you can find in a local supermarket. You can serve roasted pumpkin with air-fried bacon or eggs for the best breakfast ever!

Preparation Time	Cooking Time	Servings
5 min	38 min	4

Nutritional Information Per Serving
Energy value: 126 Kcal, Protein: 4.6g,
Carbohydrates: 15.2g, Fats: 6.4g

Ingredients
- 400g pumpkin, unpeeled
- 2 tsp. coconut oil
- 1 tsp. pumpkin spice mix
- Sea salt and ground black pepper, to taste
- 100g Ricotta cheese, crumbled
- 1 tbsp. fresh cilantro, roughly chopped
- ½ cup pomegranate seeds

Instructions
1. Cut the pumpkin into wedges and brush them with coconut oil; season with spices.
2. Place the pumpkin wedges in the lightly-greased Air Fryer cooking basket.
3. Bake the pumpkin wedges at 180°C/360°F for about 35 minutes.
4. Top the pumpkin with cheese and let it cook for a further 2 to 3 minutes. Garnish with fresh cilantro and pomegranate seeds.
5. Bon appétit!

Flapjacks with Raspberry Jam

Who doesn't love pancakes for breakfast? Start your day off right with this outstanding recipe for twisted flapjacks. They are ready in no time!

Preparation Time	Cooking Time	Servings
10 min	20 min	6

Nutritional Information Per Serving
Energy value: 436 Kcal, Protein: 8.6g,
Carbohydrates: 51.2g, Fats: 22.4g

Ingredients
- 200g old-fashioned rolled oats
- 80g caster sugar
- 100g butter
- A pinch of sea salt
- ¼ tsp. cinnamon powder
- ¼ tsp. turmeric powder
- 30g (2 tbsp.) granola
- 200g peanut butter
- 80g blackberry jam

Instructions
1. Begin by preheating your Air Fryer to 175°C/350°F. Brush your baking tin with non-stick cooking spray.
2. In your blender or food processor, mix rolled oats with sugar, butter, spices, and 100g of peanut butter. Fold in granola and gently stir to combine.
3. Spoon the batter into the prepared baking tray. Place dots of the remaining butter and jam on top of the flapjacks.
4. Bake your flapjacks for approximately 20 minutes, until golden brown. Leave your flapjacks to cool for 10 minutes before slicing and serving.
5. Bon appétit!

Bacon Egg Cups

Individual-sized mini soufflés are a cinch to make in the Air Fryer. They are flavourful and perfect for both everyday breakfasts and special occasions!

Preparation Time	Cooking Time	Servings
5 min	10 min	4

Nutritional Information Per Serving

Energy value: 223 Kcal, Protein: 12.4g, Carbohydrates: 2.2g, Fats: 17.8g

Ingredients

- 4 rashers bacon
- 4 medium eggs
- 50g Parmesan cheese, grated
- ½ tsp. red pepper flakes, crushed
- Sea salt and ground black pepper, to taste

Instructions

1. Place the bacon rashers in the muffin cases.
2. Crack 1 egg into each bacon cup. Sprinkle them with Parmesan cheese, red pepper, salt, and black pepper.
3. Bake bacon egg cups at 190°C/380°F for approximately 10 minutes, or until the eggs reach your desired level of doneness.
4. Bon appétit!

Mini Breakfast Portobellas

These mini breakfast bites are easy to make and fun to eat! Portabella mushrooms contain compounds that can fight inflammation and prevent chronic diseases.

Preparation Time	Cooking Time	Servings
5 min	6 min	3

Nutritional Information Per Serving

Energy value: 122 Kcal, Protein: 9.9g, Carbohydrates: 8.3, Fats: 6.3

Ingredients

- 3 medium Portobella mushrooms
- 1 tsp. extra-virgin olive oil
- Sea salt and ground black pepper, to taste
- ¼ tsp. cayenne pepper, or more to taste
- 3 tomato slices
- 1 garlic clove, minced
- 100g Swiss chard, shredded
- 3 medium eggs, beaten
- 30g cheddar cheese, sliced

Instructions

1. Pat dry mushroom caps using a paper towel. Toss them with olive oil, salt, black pepper, and cayenne pepper.
2. Place the mushrooms in the lightly-greased Air Fryer basket. Divide the tomato slices, garlic, and Swiss chard between mushroom cups. Top each cap with eggs and cheese.
3. Bake the stuffed portobellas in the preheated Air Fryer at 190°C/375°F for approximately 6 minutes, until eggs are set, and mushrooms are tender.
4. Bon appétit!

French Toast

This is the basic recipe for French toast. Jazz it up by adding jam, raw or canned berries, crème fraiche, or other favourite toppings.

Preparation Time	Cooking Time	Servings
5 min	15 min	2

Nutritional Information Per Serving
Energy value: 336 Kcal, Protein: 12.2g,
Carbohydrates: 32.1g, Fats: 18.3g

Ingredients
- 1 large egg
- 2 tbsp. double cream
- 2 tbsp. ground almonds
- 1 tbsp. golden caster sugar
- 1 tbsp. butter, room temperature
- 4 thick slices of white bread

Instructions
1. Begin by preheating your Air Fryer to 180°C/360°F.
2. Beat the egg with double cream until frothy. Add in ground almonds, sugar, and butter; whisk again to combine well.
3. Next, dip bread slices in the custard mixture until they are well coated on all sides.
4. Cook French toast in the preheated Air Fryer for about 15 minutes, turning halfway through the cooking time to ensure even cooking. Work in batches, if needed.
5. Enjoy!

Halloumi Fries

This Greek-inspired breakfast recipe uses simple ingredients. With its squeaky texture, halloumi can easily be cooked in your Air Fryer.

Preparation Time	Cooking Time	Servings
5 min	6 min	2

Nutritional Information Per Serving
Energy value: 356 Kcal, Protein: 19.2g,
Carbohydrates: 26.9, Fats: 19.3

Ingredients
- 200g halloumi
- 50g all-purpose flour
- 1 medium egg
- 100g crushed cornflakes
- 1 tsp. Greek seasoning mix
- 1 tsp. olive oil

Instructions
1. Cut halloumi into thick chips. Set up your breading station. Place all-purpose flour in a shallow dish. In a separate dish, whisk the egg. Combine the crushed cornflakes with Greek seasoning mix in a third dish.
2. Start by dredging halloumi pieces in the flour; then, dip them into the egg. Press halloumi into the crushed cornflakes and seasoning mix. Brush breaded halloumi pieces with olive oil.
3. Cook halloumi pieces at 190°C/375°F for about 6 minutes.
4. Serve with potato chips or your favourite dip.
5. Bon appétit!

CHAPTER 2
POULTRY

Don't Forget To Download Your Bonus PDF With The Colored Images

STEP BY STEP Guide To Access-

1. Open Your Phones (Or Any Device You Want The Book On) Back Camera. The Back Camera Is The One You use as if you are taking a picture of someone.
2. Simply point your Camera at the QR code and 'tap' the QR code with your finger to focus the camera.
3. A link / pop up will appear. Simply tap that (and make sure you have internet connection) and the FREE PDF containing all of the colored images should appear.
4. If You Click On The File And It Says 'The File Is Too Big To Preview' Simply click 'Download' and it will download the full book onto your phone!
5. Now you have access to these FOREVER. Simply 'Bookmark' The tab it opened on, or download the document and take wherever you want.
6. Repeat this on any device you want it on!

Any Issues / Feedback/ Troubleshooting please email: anthonypublishing123@gmail.com and our customer service team will help you! We want to make sure you have the BEST experience with our books!

Chicken Nuggets

This is the healthier version of famous chicken nuggets. These chicken thighs are marinated and then cooked in your Air Fryer for the best restaurant-style nuggets ever!

Preparation Time	Cooking Time	Servings
🕐	✕	🍽
10 min 3 hrs marinating	12 min	4

Nutritional Information Per Serving

Energy value: 346 Kcal, Protein: 25.2g,
Carbohydrates: 4.9g, Fats: 24.3g

Ingredients

- 500g chicken thighs, boneless, skinless
- 1 tbsp. brown mustard
- 150ml plain yogurt
- Sea salt and ground black pepper, to taste
- ¼ tsp. cayenne pepper
- ½ tsp. garlic granules
- 100g (1 cup) breadcrumbs, crushed
- 1 tbsp. olive oil

Instructions

1. Cut the chicken thighs into bite-sized pieces; then, place the chicken pieces in a ceramic (or glass) bowl; add mustard and yoghurt, and let it marinate in your fridge for about 3 hours.
2. Discard the marinade and season the chicken pieces with salt, black pepper, cayenne pepper, and garlic granules.
3. Place the breadcrumbs on a plate and roll each chicken piece onto the breadcrumbs. Brush the breaded chicken pieces with olive oil on all sides.
4. Air fry chicken nuggets at 195°C/395°F for about 12 minutes, until golden brown.
5. Enjoy!

Turkey Satay-Style Salad

Try this unique combo of air-fried turkey breasts, crunchy veggies, and zingy peanut butter sauce. This is seriously good!

Preparation Time	Cooking Time	Servings
10 min	25 min	4

Nutritional Information Per Serving

Energy value: 346 Kcal, Protein: 25.2g,
Carbohydrates: 4.9g, Fats: 24.3g

Ingredients

Salad:
- 500g turkey breast fillets
- 1 tsp. olive oil
- 2 medium Gem lettuce hearts, cut into wedges
- 1 bunch fresh coriander, chopped
- 1 small onion, thinly sliced

Sauce:
- ½ tsp. mustard seeds
- 1 tbsp. soy sauce
- ½ tsp. turmeric powder
- ½ tsp. ground cumin
- ¼ tsp. ginger powder
- 1 tsp. garlic clove, minced
- 1 tsp. agave syrup
- 1 tbsp. peanut butter
- 2 tbsp. fresh lemon juice

Instructions

1. Pat the turkey breasts dry using paper towels. Spray the turkey breasts with olive oil and arrange them in the lightly-greased cooking basket.
2. Cook the turkey breast fillets in the preheated Air Fryer at 175°C/350°F for approximately 25 minutes.
3. Turn the turkey breast fillets over and continue to cook for a further 22 to 25 minutes.
4. (Turkey breasts are done when the internal temperature reaches 73°C/165°F).
5. Meanwhile, toss the remaining salad ingredients in a salad bowl; mix all the sauce ingredients and reserve.
6. Cut the turkey breast fillets into strips and pile them on top of your salad. Dress the salad to taste and serve immediately. Devour!

Stuffed Chicken

If you find recipes for stuffed chicken complicated, you must try this air-fried stuffed chicken! This recipe will blow you away.

Preparation Time	Cooking Time	Servings
10 min	20 min	4

Nutritional Information Per Serving

Energy value: 346 Kcal, Protein: 25.2g,
Carbohydrates: 4.9g, Fats: 24.3g

Ingredients

- 500g chicken breast fillets (4 fillets)
- Sea salt and ground black pepper, to taste
- 120g mozzarella, torn into small pieces
- 1 tbsp. English mustard
- 4 smoked bacon rashers

Instructions

1. Pat the chicken dry using paper towels. Sprinkle with salt and black pepper.
2. Cut a slit into one side of each chicken fillet, making a pocket shape. Stuff the chicken with mozzarella and mustard.
3. Wrap each stuffed chicken piece with a bacon rasher and secure it with a toothpick. Repeat with the remaining ingredients.
4. Cook the stuffed chicken at 190°C/380°F for about 20 minutes, turning them over halfway through the cooking time.
5. (Chicken is done when the internal temperature reaches 75°C/167°F).
6. Enjoy!

Duck Traybake

Are you looking for a good, foolproof recipe for a family dinner? Well, then this duck traybake with herbs, tomatoes, and courgettes is a must.

Preparation Time	Cooking Time	Servings
5 min	40 min	4

Nutritional Information Per Serving

Energy value: 346 Kcal, Protein: 25.2g,
Carbohydrates: 4.9g, Fats: 24.3g

Ingredients

- 800g duck drumsticks
- 2 cloves garlic, smashed
- 2 tbsp. tomato purée
- 1 tbsp. soy sauce
- Sea salt and ground black pepper, to taste
- 2 thyme sprigs
- 1rosemary sprig
- 1 tsp. olive oil
- 200g tomatoes, diced
- 1 small courgette, sliced

Instructions

1. Toss all ingredients, except the tomatoes and zucchini, in the lightly-greased roasting tin. Lower the roasting tin into the Air Fryer cooking basket.
2. Cook the duck drumsticks at 195°C/390°F for 30 minutes.
3. Turn the duck drumsticks over and top with tomatoes and zucchini; continue to cook for another 10 minutes and serve hot.
4. Bon appétit!

Tandoori Chicken

The key to this traditional Indian dish is to use bone-in and skin-on chicken legs, since they have enough fat for air frying. Otherwise, the chicken will dry out easily.

Preparation Time	Cooking Time	Servings

5 min + 2 hrs marinating	40 min	4

Nutritional Information Per Serving

Energy value: 315 Kcal, Protein: 11.4g,
Carbohydrates: 31.4, Fats: 16.6

Ingredients
- 800g chicken leg quarters, bone-in and skin-on
- 1 tsp. olive oil
- Marinade:
- 200ml yoghurt
- 1 large lemon, freshly squeezed
- 1 tsp. fresh ginger, peeled and grated
- 2 garlic cloves, crushed
- 1 tsp. garam masala
- ½ tsp. ground coriander
- ½ tsp. turmeric powder

Instructions
1. In a ceramic bowl, place the chicken legs with all the marinade ingredients. Cover the bowl and let it marinate in your fridge for at least 2 hours. Discard the marinade.
2. Brush the marinated chicken legs with olive oil and then, arrange them in the Air Fryer cooking basket.
3. Air fry the chicken legs at 180°C/365°F for 40 minutes, flipping them halfway through the cooking time to ensure even browning.
4. Bon appétit!

Traditional Chicken Biryani

Indian-inspired food in an Air Fryer? Yes, please! Cook this traditional dish in your Air Fryer and delight your family and guests.

Preparation Time	Cooking Time	Servings

10 min 2 hrs marinating	25 min	4

Nutritional Information Per Serving

Energy value: 524 Kcal, Protein: 36.2g,
Carbohydrates: 60.5g, Fats: 19.3g

Ingredients
- 600g chicken breasts, bone-in, skinless, cut into large pieces
- 20g ghee (or butter)
- 1 bay leaf
- 1 tbsp. coriander, chopped
- 2 tbsp. curry paste
- 2 cardamom pods
- 30ml lime juice, freshly squeezed
- 1 large onion, sliced
- 200g basmati rice, cooked
- 85g raisins

Instructions
1. Place the chicken breasts, ghee (or butter), bay leaf, coriander, curry paste, cardamom, and lime juice in a ceramic bowl; cover and let it marinate for at least 2 hours in your fridge.
2. Add the marinated chicken to the lightly-greased Air Fryer cooking basket. Cook the chicken at 180°C/360°F for 12 minutes.
3. Reduce the heat to 160°C/320°F. Turn the chicken breasts over, baste with the reserved marinade, top with onion, and continue to cook for a further 10 to 12 minutes.
4. Let the chicken rest for about 5 minutes before serving. Serve over hot rice, garnished with raisins, and enjoy!

Turkey Ragù

You will love this turkey ragù with a twist! You can also add grated mozzarella on the top and let it cook for 5 minutes in your Air Fryer, until cheese has melted. Serve with pasta of your choice.

 Preparation Time **Cooking Time** **Servings**

5 min   30 min   4

Nutritional Information Per Serving

Energy value:304 Kcal, Protein: 31.2g,
Carbohydrates: 10.2g, Fats: 15.3g

Ingredients

- 20g butter, at room temperature
- 500g turkey mince
- 1 large carrot, chopped
- 1 large onion, chopped
- 1 large celery rib, chopped
- 3 cloves garlic, finely diced
- 1 tbsp. Marmite
- 1 tbsp. tomato purée
- 1 tsp. Italian seasoning mix
- 2 medium tins tomatoes, crushed

Instructions

1. Melt the butter in a non-stick frying pan over medium-high heat. Once hot, cook the turkey mince for about 5 minutes, until no longer pink. Add the remaining vegetables and continue to sauté for 5 minutes more, until tender.
2. Spoon the veg and turkey mixture into the lightly-greased baking tray and stir in the remaining ingredients; gently stir to combine.
3. Lower the baking tray into the Air Fryer cooking basket. Cook your ragù at 180°C/360°F for 20 minutes.

Baked Meatballs

If you are tired of classic meatballs, cook these flavourful balls with 2-meat combo, egg, and mozzarella. Serve the meatballs on skewers and kids will be delighted!

 Preparation Time **Cooking Time** **Servings**

5 min   20 min   4

Nutritional Information Per Serving

Energy value: 475 Kcal, Protein: 38.4g,
Carbohydrates: 8.4g, Fats: 32.3g

Ingredients

Meatballs:
- 300g turkey mince (93 % lean and 7 % fat)
- 200g pork mince (96% lean, 4% fat)
- 25g dried breadcrumbs
- 2 cloves garlic, minced
- 1 medium egg, beaten
- 1 tsp. ground cumin
- 1 tsp. red pepper flakes, crushed
- Sea salt and ground black pepper, to taste

Baked Meatballs:
- 2 (125g) balls of mozzarella, shredded

Instructions

1. In a mixing bowl, thoroughly combine all the ingredients except for the mozzarella for your meatballs. Shape the mixture into equal balls.
2. Brush the bottom of the Air Fryer cooking basket with non-stick cooking spray.
3. Air fry the meatballs at 180°C/360°F for 15 minutes. Shake the cooking basket halfway through the cooking time.
4. Top them with the mozzarella and continue to cook for 5 minutes longer, until the cheese has melted.
5. Bon appétit!

Spicy Turkey Meatloaf

An Air Fryer meatloaf is moist and tender on the inside and tangy and crispy on the outside. Let the meatloaf rest for 10 minutes before slicing. Serve with baked beans or potato mash.

Preparation Time	Cooking Time	Servings
5 min	20 min	4

Nutritional Information Per Serving

Energy value: 370 Kcal, Protein: 28.8g,
Carbohydrates: 10.7g, Fats: 23.4g

Ingredients

- 300g turkey mince (93 % lean and 7 % fat)
- 300g pork mince (96% lean, 4% fat)
- 1 medium egg, beaten
- 2 cloves garlic, minced
- 2 spring onions, sliced
- 30g dry breadcrumbs
- 1 tsp. chili powder
- Sea salt and ground black pepper, to taste
- 2 tbsp. tomato purée
- 1 tbsp. Worcestershire sauce
- 1 tbsp. honey mustard
- 5g shortening

Instructions

1. Grease a baking tin with shortening and set it aside. In a mixing bowl, thoroughly combine the minced meat, egg, garlic, onions, breadcrumbs, chili powder, salt, and black pepper. Scrape the mixture into the prepared baking tin.
2. Lower the baking tin into the Air Fryer cooking basket. Now, cook your meatloaf at 180°C/360°F for 10 minutes.
3. Meanwhile, in a small mixing bowl, thoroughly combine the tomato purée, Worcestershire sauce, and honey mustard until well combined.
4. Spread the tomato mixture over the meatloaf and bake for a further 10 minutes, until the centre of your meatloaf reaches 74°C/165°F.
5. Bon appétit!

Jerk Turkey

If you want to add an authentic Caribbean flair to your jerk turkey, use scotch bonnet chillies for the marinade. But be careful, though! These chillies may irritate your skin, so wear gloves while handling them.

Preparation Time	Cooking Time	Servings
5 min 2 hrs marinating	30 min	4

Nutritional Information Per Serving

Energy value: 246 Kcal, Protein: 43.3g,
Carbohydrates: 4g, Fats: 6.5g

Ingredients

Marinade:
- 1 chili pepper of your choice
- 2 spring onions
- 20g fresh ginger
- 3 garlic cloves
- 6 tbsp. white vinegar
- 1 tsp. ground allspice

Jerk Turkey:
- 800g turkey thighs, boneless
- 1 tsp. olive oil

Instructions

1. Make the jerk marinade – Blend all the ingredients for the marinade in your food processor or a high-speed blender; blitz to a paste and add the marinade to a ceramic (or glass) bowl.
2. Add the turkey to the bowl with the marinade, cover it, and let it marinate in your fridge for about 2 hours.
3. Brush the turkey thighs with olive oil. Cook turkey thighs in the preheated Air Fryer at 195°C/390°F for approximately 20 minutes.
4. Turn the turkey thighs over and top them with sweet onions; continue to cook for a further 10 minutes.
5. (Turkey thighs are done when the internal temperature reaches 73°C/165°F).
6. Bon appétit!

Chicken Salad with Baby Spinach

Are you ready for a fun spin on a classic chicken salad? The recipe calls for spinach, but feel free to add your favourite greens as well as other fresh veggies!

Preparation Time	Cooking Time	Servings
5 min	40 min	4

Nutritional Information Per Serving

Energy value: 298 Kcal, Protein: 48.2g,
Carbohydrates: 9.7g, Fats: 6.9

Ingredients

- 800g chicken breasts, boneless and skinless
- 2 tsp. extra-virgin olive oil
- Sea salt and ground black pepper, to taste
- 2 tsp. freshly squeezed lemon juice
- 400g baby spinach
- 100g pomegranate seeds

Instructions

1. Pat the chicken dry with paper towels; toss the chicken breasts with 1 teaspoon of olive oil, salt, and black pepper.
2. Cook the chicken at 190°C/380°F for about 40 minutes, making sure to turn them over halfway through the cooking time. Cut the chicken breasts into bite-sized pieces.
3. Toss baby spinach with the remaining 1 teaspoon of olive oil and lemon juice; transfer baby spinach to a serving platter and top with the chicken pieces.
4. Garnish your salad with pomegranate seeds and serve immediately.
5. Devour!

Easy Chicken Bake

Chicken pairs incredibly well with root vegetables and tomato sauce in this colourful Air Fryer dish. If you want saucy and crispy chicken bites, do not discard the skin. Grab warm tortillas or a homemade crusty bread for dunking.

Preparation Time	Cooking Time	Servings
5 min	40 min	4

Nutritional Information Per Serving

Energy value: 346 Kcal, Protein: 39.9g,
Carbohydrates: 3.9g, Fats: 19g

Ingredients

- 800g chicken drumsticks, cut into pieces, skin-on
- 1 tsp. olive oil
- 1 large leek, finely sliced
- 2 garlic cloves, minced
- 1 large celery rib, sliced
- 1 large carrot, trimmed and sliced
- 120ml tomato sauce
- 1 tbsp. Italian herb mix

Instructions

1. Arrange the chicken pieces in the bottom of a lightly-greased baking tin.
2. Add the other ingredients to the baking tray and gently stir to combine.
3. Bake the chicken and vegetables at 180°C/360°F for 40 minutes, until thoroughly cooked.
4. Bon appétit!

Spicy Chicken with Cherry Tomatoes

When it comes to air-fried chicken recipes, it's hard to beat an easy roasted chicken with cherry tomatoes. This poultry dish is simple but so flavourful thanks to a deep, spicy flavour and the air frying method.

Preparation Time
5 min

Cooking Time
22 min

Servings
2

Nutritional Information Per Serving

Energy value: 394 Kcal, Protein: 42.2g,
Carbohydrates: 8g, Fats: 20.2g

Ingredients

• 400g chicken breasts, cut into large pieces
• 200g cherry tomatoes
• 2 tsp. olive oil
• 1 tsp. chili powder
• Sea salt and ground black pepper, to taste

Instructions

1. Toss the chicken breasts and cherry tomatoes with olive oil and spices.
2. Arrange the chicken and tomatoes in the lightly-greased Air Fryer cooking basket. Cook the chicken and tomatoes at 180°C/360°F for 22 minutes, shaking the basket halfway through the cooking time to ensure even cooking.
3. Serve the warm chicken and garnish with cherry tomatoes. Enjoy!

Turkey Skewers

We've already cooked a lot of amazing air fryer recipes, but these turkey skewers may become your new favourite. Boneless turkey is tossed with spices and barbecue sauce, and then, they are cooked to crispy perfection. Serve with yogurt sauce.

Preparation Time
5 min

Cooking Time
25 min

Servings
4

Nutritional Information Per Serving

Energy value: 359 Kcal, Protein: 33.4g,
Carbohydrates: 2.4g, Fats: 11.5g

Ingredients

• 600g turkey breasts, boneless, cut into bite-sized pieces
• Sea salt and ground black pepper, to taste
• 30ml barbecue sauce
• ½ tsp. cayenne pepper
• ½ tsp. dried parsley flakes
• 1 tsp. olive oil
• 4 bamboo skewers soaked in water for 30 minutes

Instructions

1. Toss the turkey breasts with the other ingredients.
2. Thread the turkey pieces onto the soaked bamboo skewers and place them into the Air Fryer cooking basket.
3. Sep 3: Air fry the turkey skewers at 190°C/395°F for 25 minutes, turning them over halfway through the cooking time to ensure even browning.
4. (Turkey breasts are done when the internal temperature reaches 73°C/165°F).
5. Enjoy!

Buffalo Chicken Wings

Kick chicken wings up a notch with hot sauce, Worcestershire sauce, and honey! Marinated and cooked to perfection, Buffalo wings are the comfort food at their finest.

Preparation Time	Cooking Time	Servings
5 min + 2 hrs marinating	5 min	3

Nutritional Information Per Serving

Energy value: 366 Kcal, Protein: 29.8g,
Carbohydrates: 3.7g, Fats: 25.2g

Ingredients

- 600g chicken wings, bone-in and skin-on
- 1 tsp. olive oil
- 2 medium garlic cloves, crushed
- 2 tbsp. hot sauce
- 2 tbsp. apple cider vinegar
- 1 tsp. smoked paprika
- 1 tbsp. Worcestershire sauce
- 2 tbsp. honey

Instructions

1. In a ceramic bowl, place the chicken wings with the rest of the ingredients. Cover the bowl and let it marinate in your fridge for at least 2 hours. Discard the marinade.
2. Place the chicken wings in the lightly-greased Air Fryer cooking basket.
3. Air fry the chicken wings at 180°C/365°F for 18 to 20 minutes, flipping them halfway through cooking time to ensure even browning.
4. Bon appétit!

Chicken Legs with Carrots

Roasted chicken legs are easy to whip up, but tossing them with carrots in an Air Fryer is what makes that dish even easier. You can skip hot sauce if you're not a fan of spicy food.

Preparation Time	Cooking Time	Servings
5 min	30 min	2

Nutritional Information Per Serving

Energy value: 374 Kcal, Protein: 25.5g,
Carbohydrates: 10.3g, Fats: 25.2g

Ingredients

- 400g chicken legs, bone-in and skin on
- 200g carrots, cut into quarters lengthwise
- 1 tsp. olive oil
- 1 tbsp. hot sauce
- 1 tbsp. agave syrup
- ½ tsp. cayenne pepper
- ¼ tsp. dried dill (optional)
- Sea salt and ground black pepper, to taste

Instructions

1. Toss the chicken legs and carrots with the rest of the ingredients.
2. Place the chicken legs and carrots in the lightly-greased Air Fryer cooking basket.
3. Air fry the chicken legs at 180°C/365°F for approximately 15 minutes. Turn them over and add the carrots.
4. Continue to cook for 15 minutes longer, until everything is cooked through.
5. Bon appétit!

31

Roast Turkey

You do not have to wait for the holidays to prepare a roast turkey. An Air Fryer will allow you to cook turkey breasts whenever you want, even during busy weeknights.

Preparation Time	Cooking Time	Servings
🕐	✕	🍲
10 min	50 min	4

Nutritional Information Per Serving

Energy value: 325 Kcal, Protein: 13.9g,
Carbohydrates: 14.9, Fats: 22.8

Ingredients

Salad:
- 800g turkey breast, boneless
- 1 tsp. olive oil
- ½ tsp. mustard seeds
- ½ tsp. turmeric powder
- ½ tsp. ground cumin
- 1 tsp. agave syrup
- 2 tbsp. fresh lemon juice

Instructions

1. Pat the turkey breasts dry using paper towels. Place the turkey breasts along with the remaining ingredients in a resealable bag. Give it a good shake until the turkey breast are covered with spices on all sides.
2. Place the turkey breasts in the lightly-greased cooking basket. Cook the turkey breasts in the preheated Air Fryer at 175°C/350°F for approximately 25 minutes.
3. Turn the turkey breast over and continue to cook for a further 22 to 25 minutes.
4. (Turkey breasts are done when the internal temperature reaches 73°C/165°F).
5. Bon appétit!

Chicken Souvlaki

If you have chicken breast in your fridge, this Greek souvlaki recipe is the perfect way to use it up! You can garnish chicken souvlaki with tomatoes, cucumber, or chips.

Preparation Time	Cooking Time	Servings
🕐	✕	🍲
5 min	30 min	2

Nutritional Information Per Serving

Energy value: 566 Kcal, Protein: 48.2g,
Carbohydrates: 34.4g, Fats: 24.5g

Ingredients

- 400g chicken breasts, boneless, cut into bite-sized pieces
- Sea salt and ground black pepper, to taste
- ½ tsp. garlic granules
- Zest and juice of 1 lemon
- ½ tsp. brown mustard
- 1 tsp. olive oil
- 2 bamboo skewers (soaked in water for 30 minutes)
- 2 tbsp. tzatziki
- 2 6-inch pitta bread wraps

Instructions

1. Toss the chicken breasts with spices, lemon, mustard, and olive oil.
2. Thread the chicken pieces onto the soaked bamboo skewers; now, arrange the skewers into the Air Fryer cooking basket.
3. Air fry chicken skewers at 180°C/360°F for 25 minutes, turning them over halfway through the cooking time to ensure even browning.
4. Warm the pita bread at 160°C/320°F for approximately 5 minutes. Serve your chicken souvlaki over the pita and garnish with a generous tzatziki scoop.
5. Enjoy!

Chicken with Rosemary Potatoes

If you ever made air-fried chicken thighs and felt like they were missing something, give this recipe a try! Chicken thighs pair wonderfully with air-roasted rosemary potatoes.

Preparation Time	Cooking Time	Servings
5 min	30 min	4

Nutritional Information Per Serving

Energy value: 424 Kcal, Protein: 35.5g,
Carbohydrates: 14.5g, Fats: 25.1g

Ingredients

- 600g chicken thighs, bone-in and skin on
- 2 tsp. olive oil
- Sea salt and ground black pepper, to taste
- ½ tsp. cayenne pepper
- 300g potatoes, cut into wedges
- 1 tsp. dried rosemary

Instructions

1. Toss the chicken thighs with 1 teaspoon of olive oil, salt, black pepper, and cayenne pepper.
2. Place the chicken thighs in the lightly-greased Air Fryer cooking basket.
3. Air fry the chicken thighs at 180°C/365°F for approximately 15 minutes.
4. Toss the potato wedges with rosemary, salt, pepper and the remaining 1 teaspoon of olive oil. Turn the heat to 190°C/380°F. Turn the chicken thighs over and top them with potatoes.
5. Continue to cook for 15 minutes longer, until the chicken and potatoes are cooked through.
6. Bon appétit!

Chicken Fajitas

A chicken fajita is delicious, stripped chicken, topped with peppers, onions, and salsa, and served on tortillas. You can also use chicken leftovers to make this Tex-Mex-inspired dish.

Preparation Time	Cooking Time	Servings
5 min	22 min	4

Nutritional Information Per Serving

Energy value: 433 Kcal, Protein: 33g,
Carbohydrates: 39.3, Fats: 15.9

Ingredients

- 500g chicken breasts, skinless, boneless, and cut into 4 slices
- 2 medium bell peppers, seeded and sliced
- 1 tsp. olive oil
- Sea salt and ground black pepper, to taste
- 4 8-inch wholemeal tortillas
- 1 head of Cos/Romaine lettuce
- 1 small onion, thinly sliced
- 100g fresh salsa

Instructions

1. Toss the chicken breasts and bell peppers with olive oil and spices.
2. Lower the chicken and bell peppers into the lightly-greased Air Fryer cooking basket. Cook the chicken and bell peppers at 180°C/360°F for 22 minutes, flipping them halfway through the cooking time to ensure even cooking.
3. Cut chicken into strips. Serve warm chicken on tortillas; top with lettuce, onion, and salsa.
4. Enjoy!

Sichuan Duck Wings

While you can order this dish in any Chinese restaurant, making your own is 100% worth the effort. With your Air Fryer, it is ready in about 30 minutes. In fact, marinating is the longest part of the recipe, and after that, everything is cooked in no time!

Preparation Time	Cooking Time	Servings
5 min + 1 hr marinating	5 min	3

Nutritional Information Per Serving

Energy value: 565 Kcal, Protein: 43.7g,
Carbohydrates: 1.8g, Fats: 41.3g

Ingredients

- 1kg duck wings, boneless
- 1 teaspoon Chinese 5-spice powder
- 1 tbsp. sesame oil
- 1 tsp. maple syrup
- 2 tsp. rice wine
- 30ml orange juice
- 1 tsp dark soy sauce
- 1 tsp. garlic granules

Instructions

1. In a ceramic bowl, place the duck wings with all the ingredients. Let the duck wings marinate for about 1 hour in the fridge.
2. Cook the duck wings at 195°C/390°F for 20 minutes.
3. Turn them over, baste with the reserved marinade, and cook for a further 10 minutes. Serve hot and enjoy.
4. Bon appétit!

Glazed Duck Legs

This sumptuous recipe is perfect for your next festive dinner. Duck legs are air-roasted and covered with marmalade-based glaze. Absolute perfection!

Preparation Time	Cooking Time	Servings
10 min	15 min	4

Nutritional Information Per Serving

Energy value: 546 Kcal, Protein: 43.2g,
Carbohydrates: 2.6g, Fats: 39.1g

Ingredients

- 1kg duck leg quarters, bone-in and skin-on
- 1 tsp. olive oil

Glaze:
- 5g orange marmalade
- 1 tbsp. BBQ sauce
- 2 tbsp. tomato paste

Instructions

1. Brush the duck legs with olive oil and place them in the lightly-greased Air Fryer cooking basket.
2. Cook the duck legs at 200°C/400°F for 15 minutes, until thoroughly cooked. Meanwhile, mix all the glaze ingredients and preheat the glaze in a small saucepan.
3. Let the duck legs sit for 10 minutes before carving. Brush the hot glaze over the duck legs using a pastry brush.
4. Bon appétit!

CHAPTER 3
MEAT

**Don't Forget To Download Your Bonus PDF With
The Colored Images**

STEP BY STEP Guide To Access-

1. Open Your Phones (Or Any Device You Want The Book On) Back Camera. The Back Camera Is The One You use as if you are taking a picture of someone.
2. Simply point your Camera at the QR code and 'tap' the QR code with your finger to focus the camera.
3. A link / pop up will appear. Simply tap that (and make sure you have internet connection) and the FREE PDF containing all of the colored images should appear.
4. If You Click On The File And It Says 'The File Is Too Big To Preview' Simply click 'Download' and it will download the full book onto your phone!
5. Now you have access to these FOREVER. Simply 'Bookmark' The tab it opened on, or download the document and take wherever you want.
6. Repeat this on any device you want it on!

Any Issues / Feedback/ Troubleshooting please email: anthonypublishing123@gmail.com and our customer service team will help you! We want to make sure you have the BEST experience with our books!

Hot Spicy Meatballs

Spicy air-fried meatballs are juicy, tender, and delicious! You will knock it out of the park with your Air Fryer and this outstanding recipe!

Preparation Time	Cooking Time	Servings
5 min	15 min	4

Nutritional Information Per Serving

Energy value: 404 Kcal, Protein: 36.7g,
Carbohydrates: 14.4g, Fats: 21.5g

Ingredients
- 300g pork mince
- 300g turkey mince, 93 % lean and 7 % fat
- 1 large garlic clove, minced
- 1 small bunch flat-leaf parsley, minced
- 1 small onion, finely chopped
- 1 medium egg, beaten
- 100g fresh breadcrumbs
- ½ tsp. dry mustard
- ½ tsp. chilli flakes
- Sea salt and ground black pepper, to taste

Instructions
1. In a mixing bowl, thoroughly combine all the ingredients. Roll the mixture into golf-ball-sized meatballs.
2. Brush the bottom of the Air Fryer cooking basket with non-stick cooking spray.
3. Cook the meatballs at 180°C/360°F for 15 minutes. Make sure to shake the cooking basket halfway through the cooking time.
4. Serve the warm meatballs with cocktail toothpicks and enjoy!

Spicy Pork Chops

If you like pork chops, you will love this recipe; it is quick, simple, and oh-so-delicious! Serve these hot and spicy pork chops with pita bread and sauerkraut for the perfect air-fried meal.

Preparation Time	Cooking Time	Servings
5 min	15 min	2

Nutritional Information Per Serving

Energy value: 356 Kcal, Protein: 41.1g,
Carbohydrates: 0.1g, Fats: 19.9g

Ingredients
- 400g centre-cut pork loin chops, bone-in
- 1 tsp. olive oil
- ½ tsp. garlic granules
- ½ tsp. chilli powder
- Sea salt and ground black pepper, to taste

Instructions
1. Toss the pork loin chops in a bowl with all the ingredients. Place the pork loin chops in the Air Fryer cooking basket.
2. Air fry the pork loin chops at 190°C/375°F for about 15 minutes, until cooked through; make sure to turn them over halfway through the cooking time to ensure even browning.
3. Taste, adjust the seasoning, and serve immediately.
4. (Pork chops are done when the internal temperature reaches 63°C/145°F).
5. Enjoy!

Crackled Pork Belly

You've not had a truly crispy pork belly until you've had an air-roasted pork belly. Plus, there is no need to turn on your whole oven for this recipe. Bang!

Preparation Time	Cooking Time	Servings
5 min + marinating	50 min	6

Nutritional Information Per Serving

Energy value: 351 Kcal, Protein: 6g,
Carbohydrates: 1.3g, Fats: 35.5g

Ingredients

- 1 tbsp. coriander seeds, crushed
- ½ tsp chilli flakes
- ½ tsp. garlic granules
- Sea salt and ground black pepper, to taste
- 400g pork belly, boneless

Instructions

1. Crush the coriander seeds and chilli flakes with a pestle and mortar; add garlic granules, salt, and black pepper, and mix to combine.
2. Rub the pork skin with the spice mixture, cover it, and place in your fridge overnight.
3. Cook pork belly at 160°C/320°F for about 50 minutes until cooked through; make sure to turn the pork belly over halfway through the cooking time.
4. Enjoy!

Glazed Pork Loin

This air-roasted pork loin with sweet syrupy glaze is all you need for your next family dinner!

Preparation Time	Cooking Time	Servings
5 min	60 min	4

Nutritional Information Per Serving

Energy value: 482 Kcal, Protein: 52.5g,
Carbohydrates: 8.3g, Fats: 25.5g

Ingredients

- 900g pork loin
- 1 tsp. olive oil
- Sea salt and ground black pepper, to taste
- 100ml stout
- 2 tbsp. light muscovado sugar
- 1 tsp. chilli flakes

Instructions

1. Pat the pork loin dry with paper towels. Toss them with olive oil, salt, and black pepper.
2. Cook the pork loin at 180°C/360°F for about 30 minutes. Flip it over and continue to cook for a further 30 minutes until cooked through.
3. In the meantime, make the glaze: Place the stout, sugar, and chilli flakes in a saucepan. Cook the syrup over medium-high heat until it has reduced by almost half.
4. Carve the pork loin into slices and brush them with the prepared glaze.
5. (Pork loin is done when the internal temperature reaches 68°C/155°F).
6. Bon appétit!

Italian Meatloaf

If you like Parmesan cheese, Italian herbs, and pancetta, you must try this meatloaf in your Air Fryer. It is perfect for family gatherings, weeknight sandwiches, or picnics.

Preparation Time	Cooking Time	Servings

5 min	25 min	4

Nutritional Information Per Serving

Energy value: 37 Kcal, Protein: 38g,
Carbohydrates: 107g, Fats: 18.7g

Ingredients

- 100g pancetta, chopped
- 2 tbsp. Parmesan cheese, grated
- 300g pork mince (96% lean, 4% fat)
- 300g beef mince (95 % lean and 5 % fat)
- 1 medium egg, beaten
- 2 cloves garlic, minced
- 40g Italian seasoned breadcrumbs
- 1 tsp. Italian spice mix
- Sea salt and ground black pepper, to taste
- 2 tbsp. tomato purée

Instructions

1. In a mixing bowl, thoroughly combine the pancetta, Parmesan, minced meat, egg, garlic, breadcrumbs, Italian spice mix, salt, and black pepper. Press the mixture into the lightly-greased baking tin and smooth the top with a spatula.
2. Lower the baking tin into the Air Fryer cooking basket. Cook your meatloaf at 180°C/360°F for 15 minutes.
3. Spread the tomato purée over the meatloaf and bake it for a further 10 minutes, until nicely browned.
4. (Your meatloaf is done when the internal temperature reaches 71°C/160°F).
5. Bon appétit!

Barbecued Skirt Steak

This easy dinner for two is perfect for Valentine's Day! The secret is in the barbecued marinade that makes this steak super tender and flavourful!

Preparation Time	Cooking Time	Servings
5 min + 2 hrs marinating	18 min	2

Nutritional Information Per Serving

Energy value: 247 Kcal, Protein: 31.1g,
Carbohydrates: 4.4g, Fats: 11.7g

Ingredients

- 300g skirt steak
- 30ml barbecue sauce
- 1 tsp. olive oil
- Sea salt and ground black pepper, to taste
- 1 tsp. brown sugar

Instructions

1. Place the steak followed with all the ingredients in a ceramic or glass dish; cover the dish, and then, place it in your fridge; let it marinate for approximately 2 hours.
2. Add the steak to the lightly-greased Air Fryer cooking basket, saving the marinade for later.
3. Air fry the steak at 190°C/375°F for 16 to 18 minutes, turning it over and basting with the reserved marinade halfway through the cooking time.
4. Bon appétit!

Restaurant-Style Cheeseburger

The ultimate comfort food just got a makeover! Make homemade beef patties and cook them in your Air Fryer. This is the best-loved Air-Fryer beef recipe!

Preparation Time	Cooking Time	Servings
10 min	16 min	2

Nutritional Information Per Serving

Energy value: 464 Kcal, Protein: 37.6g,
Carbohydrates: 29.5g, Fats: 20.7g

Ingredients

- 300g beef mince (90% lean, 10% fat)
- 1 tsp. olive oil
- 1 small onion, finely chopped
- 1 garlic clove, finely chopped
- 1 tbsp. fresh cilantro, minced
- Sea salt and ground black pepper, to taste
- ½ tsp. smoked paprika
- 40g Cheddar cheese (2 slices)
- 2 hamburger buns

Instructions

1. Mix the beef mince, olive oil, onion, garlic, cilantro, salt, black pepper, and smoked paprika until everything is well incorporated.
2. Shape your mix into 2 equal-sized patties. Lower the patties into the lightly-greased Air Fryer cooking basket.
3. Cook the patties at 180°C/360°F for 10 minutes.
4. Flip the patties over, top with cheese, and continue to cook for 6 minutes on the other side, until the cheese has melted.
5. Serve the warm patties on your hamburger buns and garnish with your favourite toppings.
6. Enjoy!

Sticky Ribs

These air-fried ribs pack a sweet and spicy punch. Use dry red wine, English mustard, and dried herbs for the marinade, and watch the magic happen!

Preparation Time	Cooking Time	Servings
5 min + 2hrs marinating	35 min	3

Nutritional Information Per Serving

Energy value: 344 Kcal, Protein: 32.1g,
Carbohydrates: 3.1g, Fats: 26.6g

Ingredients

- 400g chuck short ribs
- 1 tsp. Worcestershire sauce
- 1 tsp. hot mustard
- 1 tsp. olive oil
- 1 tsp. honey
- ½ tsp. red pepper flakes, crushed
- 1 tsp. dried rosemary
- Coarse sea salt and ground black pepper, to taste

Instructions

1. Add all ingredients to a large resealable bag. Give it a good shake and let the ribs marinate in your fridge for about 2 hours.
2. Remove the ribs from the marinade and transfer them to the lightly-greased Air Fryer cooking basket.
3. Cook the ribs in the preheated Air Fryer at 200°C/395°F for 15 minutes. Turn the ribs over, baste them with the reserved marinade, and cook for 15 to 20 minutes more.
4. Serve warm and enjoy!

Sausage & Pepper Pilaf

This Air Fryer pilaf is packed with aromas, thanks to the roasted sausage and bell peppers. Pilaf goes with almost anything, from fresh lettuce to pickled vegetables.

Preparation Time	Cooking Time	Servings
45 min	15 min	4

Nutritional Information Per Serving

Energy value: 276 Kcal, Protein: 9.1g,
Carbohydrates: 18.1g, Fats: 18.2g

Ingredients

- 200g pork sausage, casing removed
- 2 bell peppers, seeded
- 1 tsp. brown mustard
- 2 tsp. olive oil
- 200g cooked white long-grain rice
- 1 small onion, sliced
- Coarse sea salt and ground black pepper, to taste

Instructions

1. Cut the pork sausages and peppers into slices; toss them with brown mustard and 1 teaspoon of olive oil.
2. Cook the pork sausages and peppers in the preheated Air Fryer at 200°C/395°F for 10 minutes, shaking the basket halfway through the cooking time.
3. Add the remaining 1 teaspoon of olive oil, rice, and onion to the baking tray; stir in the reserved sausages and peppers. Season with salt and black pepper and gently stir to combine.
4. Bake your pilaf for 5 minutes longer, until thoroughly cooked.
5. Bon appétit!

Easy Wonton Cups

Are you looking for a healthier alternative to deep-fried wontons? Check out this recipe for crispy, golden-brown wonton cups with a Mexican flair!

Preparation Time	Cooking Time	Servings
5 min	12 min	6

Nutritional Information Per Serving

Energy value: 187 Kcal, Protein: 11.1g,
Carbohydrates: 14.7g, Fats: 8.7g

Ingredients

- 200g beef mince (96% lean, 4% fat), browned and drained
- 2 spring onions, chopped
- 1 pack of taco seasoning
- 50ml canned tomatoes with chillies, diced and drained
- 18 (10-cm) wonton wrappers
- 60g cheddar cheese, grated

Instructions

1. Thoroughly combine the beef, onion, seasoning mix, and tomatoes. Brush 18 muffin cases with non-stick oil.
2. Next, line muffin cases with wonton wrappers. Divide the beef filling between wonton wrappers; top with the cheese, and then, press the edges together to seal using wet hands.
3. Bake your wontons at 185°C/370°F for 12 minutes, until they are hot and golden. Work in batches.
4. Bon appétit!

Pork Hot Pot

You can add some red chili pepper flakes in addition to other spices in this recipe. Serve over hot rice and enjoy!

Preparation Time	Cooking Time	Servings
5 min + 2 hrs marinating	30 min	4

Nutritional Information Per Serving

Energy value: 345 Kcal, Protein: 23.5g,
Carbohydrates: 5.6g, Fats: 25g

Ingredients

- 400g rib eye steak, thinly sliced
- 1 tbsp olive oil
- 2 tbsp. hoisin sauce
- 2 tbsp. rice vinegar
- 1 tbsp. grated ginger
- 2 tbsp. cornmeal
- 1 medium onion, peeled and sliced
- 1 red pepper, seeded and halved
- 1 garlic clove, finely sliced
- 100g Canadian bacon, sliced

Instructions

1. Place the rib eye steaks, olive oil, hoisin sauce, vinegar, and ginger in a ceramic dish; cover and allow it to marinate for approximately 2 hours in your fridge. Discard the marinade.
2. Toss the marinated steaks with the cornmeal and add them to the lightly-greased baking tin.
3. Add the rest of the ingredients to the baking tin. Next, cover the baking tin with foil (shiny side down). Add the baking tin to the Air Fryer cooking basket.
4. Cook the steaks and vegetables at 180°C/360°F for about 30 minutes. Enjoy!

Beef Wellington

As the perfect holiday dish, a twisted beef Wellington may become another family favourite! Everything is better with puff pastry, right?!

Preparation Time	Cooking Time	Servings
5 min	30 min	4

Nutritional Information Per Serving

Energy value: 686 Kcal, Protein: 32.1g,
Carbohydrates: 33.6g, Fats: 45g

Ingredients

- 10g butter
- 100g button mushrooms, chopped
- 1 medium onion, finely chopped
- 500g beef mince (85 % lean and 15 % fat)
- 50g tomato ketchup
- 2 eggs
- Sea salt and ground black pepper, to taste
- 1 tbsp. parsley, chopped
- 2 garlic cloves, finely chopped
- 250g pack puff pastry

Instructions

1. Melt the butter in a frying pan over a medium-high flame. Sauté the mushrooms and onions for about 3 minutes until tender; put aside for later.
2. Thoroughly combine the beef, ketchup, one egg, seasoning, and garlic. (You can use a table-top mixer or a food processor).
3. Next, roll the meat into a log(meatloaf) and place it in a lightly-greased baking tray. Bake the meatloaf at 180°C/360°F for 15 minutes.
4. Meanwhile, beat the remaining egg with a little water.
5. Roll puff pastry into a rectangle. Spread the onion/mushroom mix along the middle of the rectangle. Place the prepared meatloaf on top and fold the pastry; brush with the egg wash and place the Beef Wellington on the baking tray.
6. Bake your Beef Wellington at 180°C/360°F for 15 minutes, until golden-brown. Bon appétit!

Pork Carnitas

You will love the combination of flavours in this Mexican classic dish. It brings together pork tenderloin, chipotle sauce, and seeds! You can use substitute hamburger rolls with tortillas of your choice.

Preparation Time	Cooking Time	Servings
5 min	22 min	3

Nutritional Information Per Serving

Energy value: 315 Kcal, Protein: 11.4g,
Carbohydrates: 31.4, Fats: 16.6

Ingredients
- 1 tsp. fennel seeds
- 1 tsp. chilli flakes
- ½ tsp. mustard seeds
- 400g pork tenderloin
- 1 tsp. olive oil
- Sea salt and ground black pepper, to taste
- 4 tbsp. chipotle sauce
- 3 medium tortillas

Instructions
1. Crush the fennel seeds, chilli flakes, and mustard seeds with a pestle and mortar; set it aside.
2. Pat the pork tenderloin dry using paper towels. Rub the pork tenderloin with olive oil, spice mixture, salt, and pepper.
3. Cook the pork tenderloin at 180°C/360°F for about 12 minutes. Turn the meat over, brush it with the chipotle sauce, and continue to cook for a further 10 minutes or until cooked through.
4. Discard the skin and shred the pork using two forks.
5. (Pork tenderloin is done when the internal temperature reaches 68°C/155°F).
6. Add shredded pork to the warm tortillas, garnish with the remaining chipotle sauce, and enjoy!

Roast Pork

You can grill pork outside, but if it's cold, you can use your Air Fryer. If you want pork shoulder that falls apart at the touch of the fork, let it sit in your fridge overnight.

Preparation Time	Cooking Time	Servings
10 min + marinating	25 min	2

Nutritional Information Per Serving

Energy value: 422 Kcal, Protein: 62gg,
Carbohydrates: 2.2g, Fats: 17.5g

Ingredients
- 500g pork shoulder, boneless
- 1 tsp. olive oil
- 1 tsp. cayenne pepper
- Coarse sea salt and ground black pepper, to taste

Instructions
1. Pat the pork shoulder dry with paper towels. Score the rind (about 1 cm deep). Next, rub the pork with olive oil, cayenne pepper, salt, and black pepper; let it rest overnight in your fridge.
2. Transfer the pork shoulder to the Air Fryer cooking basket. Cook the pork shoulder at 200°C/400°F for about 25 minutes.
3. Let it rest on a carving board for about 10 minutes before serving.
4. Bon appétit!

Asian Sweet and Sour Pork

Are you looking for a pork roast that's ready in a flash? Allow the Boston butt to marinate in this Asian-inspired sweet and sour mix, and cook it in your Air Fryer for about 25 minutes.

Preparation Time	Cooking Time	Servings
10 min + 1 hr marinating	25 min	3

Nutritional Information Per Serving

Energy value: 382 Kcal, Protein: 29.9g,
Carbohydrates: 9g, Fats: 24.1g

Ingredients

- 600g Boston butt, boneless
- 2 tbsp. rice vinegar
- 1 tbsp. soy sauce
- 1 tsp. sesame oil
- 1 tbsp. honey
- 1 tbsp. peanut butter
- 2 tbsp. tomato sauce
- Ground black pepper, to taste

Instructions

1. Use paper towels to pat Boston butt dry. Score the skin of the Boston butt using a sharp knife. Mix all other ingredients until well combined; rub this sweet and sour mixture all over the outside; let it rest for about 1 hour in your fridge.
2. Transfer the Boston butt to the Air Fryer cooking basket. Cook the Boston butt at 200°C/400°F for about 25 minutes.
3. Let it rest for approximately 10 minutes before carving and serving.
4. Bon appétit!

Meatball Sliders

These meatball sliders are packed with flavours, stuffed with cheese and smoky barbecue sauce and baked to perfection in your Air Fryer. Use a chipotle sauce for even better results!

Preparation Time	Cooking Time	Servings
5 min	20 min	4

Nutritional Information Per Serving

Energy value: 404 Kcal, Protein: 36.7g,
Carbohydrates: 14.4g, Fats: 21.5g

Ingredients
Meatballs:
- 200g beef mince (93% lean and 7% fat)
- 300g pork mince
- 1 small onion, finely chopped
- 1 small bell pepper, seeded and chopped
- 1 garlic clove, minced
- 1 small bunch cilantro, chopped
- 1 medium egg, beaten
- 100g fresh breadcrumbs
- ½ tsp. smoked paprika
- Sea salt and ground black pepper, to taste

Meatball Sliders:
- 4 tbsp. smoky barbecue sauce
- 8 mini rolls
- 80g (8 slices) cheddar cheese

Instructions

1. In a mixing bowl, thoroughly combine all the ingredients for the meatballs. Roll the mixture into 8 meatballs.
2. Brush the bottom of the Air Fryer cooking basket with non-stick cooking spray.
3. Cook the meatballs at 180°C/360°F for 15 minutes, shaking the cooking basket halfway through the cooking time.
4. Spread barbecue sauce on mini rolls and top them with meatballs. Top them with the cheese and bake meatball sliders for 5 minutes, until the cheese has melted.
5. Serve warm and enjoy!

Fall-off-the-Bone Spare Ribs

Tender ribs, tomato ketchup, and hot sauce join together to make a pork dish that tastes just as good as famous restaurant versions! Wow your family and thank me later!

Preparation Time
5 min + 2 hrs marinating

Cooking Time
25 min

Servings
4

Nutritional Information Per Serving

Energy value: 284 Kcal, Protein: 33.1g,
Carbohydrates: 15.1g, Fats: 9.9g

Ingredients

- 600g spare ribs
- 100ml tomato ketchup
- 1 tsp. olive oil
- 1 tsp. soy sauce
- 1 tsp. hot sauce
- 1 tsp. honey
- 1 tsp. garlic granules
- 1 tsp. onion granules
- Sea salt and ground black pepper, to taste

Instructions

1. Add all ingredients to a ceramic dish. Cover the dish and let the ribs marinate in your fridge for about 2 hours (or overnight).
2. Remove the ribs from the marinade and transfer them to the lightly-greased Air Fryer cooking basket. Reserve the marinade.
3. Cook the ribs in the preheated Air Fryer at 200°C/395°F for 15 minutes. Turn the ribs over, baste them with the reserved marinade, and cook for an extra 20 minutes.
4. Serve warm and enjoy!

Pork Sandwiches

This air-fryer pork sandwich may become your go-to dinner during busy weeknights. If you end up with leftovers, you can reheat the pork in the Air Fryer at 150°C/305°F for about 5 minutes for a delicious snack.

Preparation Time
5 min

Cooking Time
20 min

Servings
2

Nutritional Information Per Serving

Energy value: 434 Kcal, Protein: 50.5g,
Carbohydrates: 29.3g, Fats: 11.5g

Ingredients

- 400g pork loin
- 1 tsp. olive oil
- ½ tsp. ground cumin
- ½ tsp. cayenne pepper
- Sea salt and ground black pepper, to taste
- 4 tbsp. good smoky barbecue sauce
- 2 soft white rolls

Instructions

1. Pat the pork loin dry with paper towels. Toss them with olive oil and spices.
2. Cook the pork loin at 180°C/360°F for about 25 minutes. Turn them over, baste with the barbecue sauce, and continue to cook for a further 25 minutes, until cooked through.
3. Cut the skin off and shred the pork using two forks; make sure to ditch fatty bits.
4. (Pork loin is done when the internal temperature reaches 68°C/155°F).
5. Serve shredded pork in white rolls and enjoy!

Steak with Cherry Tomatoes

Would you like to know the secret to a perfectly cooked steak with roasted cherry tomatoes? Marinate your steak and toss it in your Air Fryer for about 18 minutes. Enjoy!

Preparation Time	Cooking Time	Servings

5 min + 2 hrs marinating	18 min	3

Nutritional Information Per Serving

Energy value: 315 Kcal, Protein: 36.1g,
Carbohydrates: 5g, Fats: 15.6g

Ingredients

- 500g bavette (flank) steak
- 10ml soy sauce
- 1 tbsp. Dijon mustard
- 1 tsp. olive oil
- Sea salt and ground black pepper, to taste
- 1 tsp. honey
- 6 cherry tomatoes

Instructions

1. Place all the ingredients in a ceramic dish; cover and allow it to marinate for approximately 2 hours in your fridge.
2. Add the steak to the lightly-greased Air Fryer cooking basket, reserving the marinade. Air fry the steak at 180°C/360°F for 8 minutes. Next, turn it over, baste it with the reserved marinade, and add cherry tomatoes to the cooking basket.
3. Continue to cook the steak and cherry tomatoes for a further 10 minutes, until thoroughly cooked.
4. (Steak is done when the internal temperature reaches 75°C/167°F for well done or 65°C/150°F for medium).
5. Bon appétit!

Cheesy Pork Fillet

When you think of cheese and meat, it doesn't get any better than cheesy, melt-in-your-mouth pork with mozzarella. You can use leftovers to make sandwiches or pack your lunch box.

Preparation Time	Cooking Time	Servings
5 min	20 min	2

Nutritional Information Per Serving

Energy value: 422 Kcal, Protein: 62.g,
Carbohydrates: 2.2g, Fats: 17.5g

Ingredients

- 500g pork loin
- 1 tsp. olive oil
- Sea salt and ground black pepper, to taste
- ½ tsp. dried parsley flakes
- 1 tbsp. Dijon mustard
- 1 tsp. chilli flakes
- 50g mozzarella cheese, shredded

Instructions

1. Pat the pork loin dry with paper towels. Toss the pork with olive oil, salt, black pepper, dried parsley, mustard, and chilli flakes.
2. Cook the pork loin at 180°C/360°F for about 25 minutes. Turn it over and continue to cook for a further 20 minutes.
3. Top with cheese and continue to cook for a further 5 minutes until cheese has melted.
4. Bon appétit!

Pork Chops with Peppers

Air Fryer newbies love a good meat and vegetables combination. Pork chops pair wonderfully with bell peppers; the flavours complement each other, and the dish looks delicious! It's what your perfect meal dreams are made of!

Preparation Time	Cooking Time	Servings
5 min	15 min	4

Nutritional Information Per Serving

Energy value: 31 Kcal, Protein: 30.9g,
Carbohydrates: 2.4g, Fats: 17.7g

Ingredients

- 600g pork chops, bone-in
- 2 bell peppers, deveined
- 1 tsp. olive oil
- 1 tsp. wholegrain mustard
- ¼ tsp. cumin, ground
- ½ tsp. garlic granules
- Sea salt and ground black pepper, to taste

Instructions

1. Pat the pork chops dry with paper towels. Cut the peppers into halves. Then, place the pork and peppers in a large resealable bag, followed by the other ingredients. Give it a good shake until the pork chops are well coated with spices on all sides.
2. Place the pork chops and bell peppers in the Air Fryer cooking basket. Cook the pork chops and peppers at 190°C/375°F for about 15 minutes. Make sure to flip them over halfway through the cooking time to ensure even cooking.
3. (Always cook pork chops to 63°C/145°F).
4. Serve warm and enjoy!

Pork Medallions

This recipe calls for lard, which is a highly versatile fat for air frying. With smoke point of 190 degrees C, it won't smoke at high temperatures, which makes it the perfect choice for this dish!

Preparation Time	Cooking Time	Servings
5 min	15 min	4

Nutritional Information Per Serving

Energy value: 241 Kcal, Protein: 28.9g,
Carbohydrates: 7.7g, Fats: 9.7g

Ingredients

- 600 pork medallions
- 1 tsp. lard (olive oil)
- 1 tsp. maple syrup
- 1 tsp. garlic granules
- 1 tsp. onion granules
- ½ tsp. dried chilli flakes

Instructions

1. Pat the pork medallions dry with paper towels. Next, toss the pork medallions with the rest of the ingredients.
2. Place the pork medallions in the Air Fryer cooking basket. Cook the pork medallions at 190°C/375°F for about 15 minutes or until browned, turning them over halfway through the cooking time.
3. Serve warm and enjoy!

CHAPTER 4 FISH & SEAFOOD

**Don't Forget To Download Your Bonus PDF With
The Colored Images**

STEP BY STEP Guide To Access-

1. Open Your Phones (Or Any Device You Want The Book On) Back Camera. The Back Camera Is The One You use as if you are taking a picture of someone.
2. Simply point your Camera at the QR code and 'tap' the QR code with your finger to focus the camera.
3. A link / pop up will appear. Simply tap that (and make sure you have internet connection) and the FREE PDF containing all of the colored images should appear.
4. If You Click On The File And It Says 'The File Is Too Big To Preview' Simply click 'Download' and it will download the full book onto your phone!
5. Now you have access to these FOREVER. Simply 'Bookmark' The tab it opened on, or download the document and take wherever you want.
6. Repeat this on any device you want it on!

Any Issues / Feedback/ Troubleshooting please email: anthonypublishing123@gmail.com and our customer service team will help you! We want to make sure you have the BEST experience with our books!

Fish and Chips

When it comes to Air Fryer chips, it's all about achieving a good balance with the oil – not too greasy, not too dry. Do not forget to shake the cooking basket a couple of times to ensure even cooking.

Preparation Time	Cooking Time	Servings
10 min	35 min	3

Nutritional Information Per Serving

Energy value: 571 Kcal, Protein: 44.8g,
Carbohydrates: 74.4g, Fats: 10.2g

Ingredients
- 450g (3 fillets) tilapia fish
- 300g potatoes, peeled and cut into chips
- 2 tsp. olive oil
- 1 large egg, beaten
- Sea salt and ground black pepper, to taste
- 130g self-raising flour
- 130g fresh breadcrumbs
- 1 tsp. Cajun seasoning

Instructions
1. Pat the fish fillets dry using paper towels.
2. Coat the potato chips with 1 teaspoon of olive oil and transfer them to the Air Fryer cooking basket. Next, air fry your chips at 180°C/360°F for about 20 minutes, shaking the basket halfway through the cooking time.
3. Step 3 Make the breading station: Beat the egg until pale and frothy. In a separate shallow dish, mix the salt, pepper, and flour. In a third shallow dish, thoroughly combine the breadcrumbs with Cajun seasoning.
4. Dip fish fillets in the egg batter, then, dip them in the flour mixture until they are well coated on all sides. Roll them over the breadcrumb mix. Brush fish fillets with the remaining teaspoon of olive oil and place them in the Air Fryer cooking basket.
5. Cook the fish fillets at 200°C/400°degrees F for 6 minutes; turn the fillets over and cook for an extra 6 minutes.
6. Serve warm and enjoy your homemade fish and chips!

Roast Fish

An Italian spice mix makes everything better! You can make your homemade version by mixing oregano, basil, rosemary, marjoram, and thyme. Devour!

Preparation Time	Cooking Time	Servings
10 min	12 min	3

Nutritional Information Per Serving

Energy value: 145 Kcal, Protein: 26.3g,
Carbohydrates: 2.5g, Fats: 2.8g

Ingredients
- 400g pollock fillets, skinless
- 1 tsp. dried Italian spice mix
- Sea salt and ground black pepper, to your liking
- 1 tsp. olive oil
- 1 small lemon, cut into wedges
-

Instructions
1. Pat pollock fillets dry using paper towels. Coat the pollock fillets with spices and olive oil.
2. Cook the fillets at 200°C/400°degrees F for 6 minutes; turn the fillets over and cook for a further 6 minutes.
3. Garnish the warm fish with lemon wedges and enjoy!

Grilled Lobster Tails

Try this decadent seafood dish that is made with lobster tails and herb butter. Don't let the fancy title fool you; thanks to your Air Fryer, the lobster tails come together quickly and effortlessly.

Preparation Time
10 min

Cooking Time
12 min

Servings
2

Nutritional Information Per Serving

Energy value: 145 Kcal, Protein: 26.3g,
Carbohydrates: 2.5g, Fats: 2.8g

Ingredients

- 2 lobster tails, fresh or frozen (and defrosted)
- 60g butter, at room temperature
- 1 garlic clove, crushed
- 1 tbsp. fresh parsley leaves, finely chopped
- 1 tbsp. fresh cilantro leaves, finely chopped
- 1 tsp. spicy mustard
- Sea salt and ground black pepper, to taste
- 1 small lemon, preferably freshly squeezed

Instructions

- Prepare the lobster tails: Rinse the lobster tails and use kitchen scissors (or a sharp knife) to open the shells and remove the vein and fins.
- Grease the Air Fryer cooking basket with 1 teaspoon of butter. Lower the lobster tails into the cooking basket. Cook the lobster tails at 195°C/380°degrees F for 6 minutes.
- While the lobster tails are cooking, mix the butter with the other ingredients.
- Top the lobster tails with the butter mixture, and cook for a further 6 minutes, until cooked through.
- Bon appétit!

Swordfish Steak

Once you've had an air-fried swordfish, you will always prepare it this way. Marinating is the best way to cook fish steak that is incredibly juicy on the inside and golden on the outside.

Preparation Time
5 min + 1 hr marinating

Cooking Time
12 min

Servings
3

Nutritional Information Per Serving

Energy value: 245 Kcal, Protein: 27.3g,
Carbohydrates: 3.2g, Fats: 10.4g

Ingredients

- 400g swordfish steaks, 2cm thick
- 100ml dry white wine
- 20ml soy sauce
- 2 garlic cloves, crushed
- 1 bay leaf
- 4 fresh mint leaves
- 1 tsp. extra-virgin olive oil
- 1 lemon, cut into wedges

Instructions

1. Place the swordfish steaks in a ceramic dish along with the wine, soy sauce, garlic, bay leaf, mint, and olive oil; cover it and let it marinate for about 1 hour in the fridge.
2. Remove the swordfish steaks from the marinade and transfer it to the cooking basket; discard the marinade.
3. Cook the swordfish steaks at 200°C/395° F for 6 minutes; turn the steak over and cook for a further 6 minutes.
4. Garnish swordfish steaks with lemon wedges and enjoy!

Festive Haddock Gratin

This is a perfect blend of flavours that will delight your taste buds: smoked fish, spinach, butter, crème fraiche, and Parmesan cheese. You can also use double cream, cream cheese, or cheddar cheese. Devour!

Preparation Time	Cooking Time	Servings
5 min	17 min	4

Nutritional Information Per Serving

Energy value: 494 Kcal, Protein: 45.2g,
Carbohydrates: 24.2g, Fats: 24.4g

Ingredients
- 400g spinach, cleaned and cut into pieces
- 20g butter
- 2 spring onions, sliced
- ½ tsp. cayenne pepper
- Sea salt and ground black pepper, to taste
- 500g smoked haddock, skinless, cut into 4 pieces

Topping:
- 200ml crème fraiche
- 100g Parmesan cheese, grated
- A pinch of freshly grated nutmeg
- 50g dried breadcrumbs

Instructions
1. Add the spinach to an over-the-sink colander. Pour over a kettleful of hot water to wilt the spinach leaves. Then, rinse and squeeze out as much liquid from the spinach as you can.
2. Butter a gratin dish and spread the spinach on the bottom. Add green onions, and sprinkle them with cayenne pepper, salt, and black pepper. Nestle the haddock pieces in the vegetables.
3. Air Fry your gratin at 185°C/370° F for approximately 10 minutes.
4. Mix crème fraiche, cheese, and nutmeg. Add the mix, followed by the breadcrumbs, and bake your gratin for a further 7 minutes. Bon appétit!

Cajun Shrimp

Shrimp cooks up super quickly in your Air Fryer. Layer pita wedges with hummus, tomatoes, greens, and finish with the shrimp for a satisfying seafood dish.

Preparation Time	Cooking Time	Servings
5 min	6 min	4

Nutritional Information Per Serving

Energy value: 333 Kcal, Protein: 30.3g,
Carbohydrates: 37.7g, Fats: 7.6g

Ingredients
- 500g extra-large shrimp, peeled and deveined
- 1 tbsp. Cajun spice mix
- 20g mayonnaise
- 200 ml buttermilk
- 50g polenta
- 150g cornmeal
- 1 garlic clove, crushed
- 4 fresh lemon slices

Instructions
1. Toss your shrimp with the Cajun spice mix. Thoroughly combin the mayonnaise and buttermilk in a bowl. In a separate bow mix the polenta, cornmeal, and garlic.
2. Dip your shrimp in the buttermilk mixture; now, coat them i the polenta mixture.
3. Cook your shrimp at 200°C/395° F for 6 minutes, shakin the basket halfway through the cooking time to ensure eve browning.
4. Garnish your shrimp with lemon wedges and enjoy!

Tuna Niçoise Salad

Adding air-fried tuna with air-fried eggs, vegs, and olives to a salad bowl makes for a flavourful dinner everyone will love. Perfect for cheese lovers, the dish can be adorned with feta cheese.

Preparation Time	Cooking Time	Servings
5 min	27 min	4

Nutritional Information Per Serving

Energy value: 252 Kcal, Protein: 32.1g,
Carbohydrates: 2.8g, Fats: 11.6g

Ingredients

- 500g tuna fillets
- 2 tsp. extra-virgin olive oil
- 2 large eggs
- 1 small red onion, sliced into rings
- 1 medium tomato, cut into wedges
- 1 handful mixed greens
- 7-8 black olives, pitted
- 1 tsp. dried oregano
- 1 tbsp. apple cider vinegar

Instructions

Pat the tuna fillets dry with paper towels. Brush the fillets with 1 teaspoon of olive oil and lower them into the cooking basket. Cook the tuna fillets at 200°C/395° F for 6 minutes; turn the fillets over and continue to cook for 6 minutes more.

Add the wire rack to the Air Fryer cooking basket; carefully arrange the eggs on the rack. Air fry the eggs at 130°C/270°F for 15 minutes until set. Peel the eggs and cut them into slices. Cut the fish into strips and transfer them to a nice salad bowl. Add the eggs, onion, tomato, mixed greens, olives, and oregano to the salad bowl. Drizzle the salad with the remaining olive oil and apple cider vinegar. Enjoy!

Fish Fingers

Make the most out of the cod fish using your Air Fryer and a few simple ingredients. While the fish is cooking, make the mayo sauce that adds zest to any ordinary dish.

Preparation Time	Cooking Time	Servings
5 min	15 min	2

Nutritional Information Per Serving

Energy value: 396 Kcal, Protein: 31.5g,
Carbohydrates: 18.7g, Fats: 18g

Ingredients

- 300g cod fish, skinless
- 1 medium egg
- 60g seasoned breadcrumbs
- 40g mayonnaise
- 20ml plain yoghurt
- 1 spring onion, chopped

Instructions

1. Pat the fish dry using paper towels and cut it into 9 strips. Brush the bottom of the cooking basket with non-stick cooking oil.
2. Beat the egg until frothy and tip the breadcrumbs onto another plate.
3. Dip the fish strips into the egg wash; now, roll them onto the seasoned breadcrumbs. Arrange the prepared fish fingers in the cooking basket and brush them with non-stick oil.
4. Cook the fish fingers at 200°C/400°F for 15 minutes, until golden. In the meantime, mix the other ingredients. Serve the fish fingers with the mayo sauce and enjoy!

Tangy Sea Scallops

Mix freshly ground spices with extra-virgin olive oil and freshly squeezed lemon juice to make the best rub for your seafood. Serve warm sea scallops with a chilli sauce on the side.

Preparation Time	Cooking Time	Servings
5 min	7 min	4

Nutritional Information Per Serving

Energy value: 133 Kcal, Protein: 18.7g,
Carbohydrates: 8.5g, Fats: 2.3g

Ingredients

- 1 knob of fresh root ginger, peeled
- 1 tsp. celery seeds
- 1 tsp. mustard seeds
- 1 large garlic, peeled
- Sea salt and ground black pepper, to taste
- 1 medium lemon, freshly squeezed
- 1 tsp. extra-virgin olive oil
- 600g sea scallops

Instructions

1. Crush the ginger, celery seeds, mustard seeds, and garlic using a pestle and mortar. Then, add salt, black pepper, lemon, and olive oil, and mix to combine well.
2. Rub the scallops with the spice mixture and arrange them in the cooking basket.
3. Air fry the scallops at 200°C/395° F for 7 minutes, shaking the basket halfway through the cooking time.

Spicy Tiger Prawns

Cooking tiger prawns in an Air Fryer requires little effort, with minimal risk of the food sticking to the bottom of the pan. Serve over the hot pasta of your choice.

Preparation Time	Cooking Time	Servings
5 min	6 min	2

Nutritional Information Per Serving

Energy value: 132 Kcal, Protein: 13.7g,
Carbohydrates: 3g, Fats: 7.1g

Ingredients

- 15 g butter, at room temperature
- 200g raw tiger prawns, peeled and deveined
- 1 garlic clove, crushed
- 30 ml sherry wine
- 1 medium lemon, freshly squeezed
- ½ tsp. cayenne pepper, or more to your liking
- Sea salt and ground black pepper, to your liking

Instructions

1. Place the tiger prawns with the other ingredients in a resealabl bag. Give it a good shake until all prawns are well coated wit spices.
2. Cook tiger prawns at 200°C/395° F for 6 minutes, shaking th basket halfway through the cooking time.
3. Serve over hot spaghetti and enjoy!

Saucy Sea Bass

Sea Bass has a mild fish taste with a subtle sweetness; thus, non-fish eaters will love this recipe. The best alternatives for sea bass include cod, grouper, or tilapia.

Preparation Time	Cooking Time	Servings
10 min	13 min	3

Nutritional Information Per Serving

Energy value: 166 Kcal, Protein: 24.9g,
Carbohydrates: 4.5g, Fats: 4.2g

Ingredients

- 3(about 150g each) sea bass fillets, skin on, scaled
- 1 small knob of ginger, peeled
- 3 garlic cloves, peeled
- 1 tsp. olive oil
- 1 tbsp. fish sauce
- 3 tbsp. dry white wine
- Sea salt and ground black pepper, to taste
- 1 tsp. red pepper flakes
- ½ tsp. dried oregano

Instructions

1. Pat the sea bass fillets dry using paper towels. Crush the peeled ginger and garlic using a garlic press.
2. Toss the sea bass fillets with the ginger-garlic mixture followed by the other ingredients.
3. Cook the sea bass fillets at 190°C/370°degrees F for 7 minutes; turn the fillets over and cook for a further 6 minutes.
4. Bon appétit!

Crab Croquettes

You can use white and brown crabmeat for this recipe. When it comes to the potatoes, floury potatoes, such as King Edward or Maris Piper work best.

Preparation Time	Cooking Time	Servings
35 min	30 min	4

Nutritional Information Per Serving

Energy value: 329 Kcal, Protein: 20.2g,
Carbohydrates: 48.9g, Fats: 5.6g

Ingredients

- 400g Maris Piper potatoes, peeled and diced
- 2 tsp. olive oil
- Sea salt and ground black pepper, to your liking
- 2 spring onions, finely chopped
- 250g crabmeat
- ½ tsp. dried dill (optional)
- ½ tsp. dried oregano (optional)
- 1 tsp. dried parsley flakes
- 1 tsp. lemon zest
- 60g plain flour
- 1 medium egg, beaten
- 100g dried breadcrumbs

Instructions

1. Toss the potatoes with 1 teaspoon of olive oil, salt, and pepper.
2. Place the potatoes in the Air Fryer cooking basket and cook them at 190°C/380°F for about 10 minutes; shake the basket and continue cooking for 10 to 12 minutes more, until they are thoroughly cooked.
3. Push the potatoes through a ricer. Stir in the onions, crabmeat, herbs, and lemon zest. Stir until well combined, and shape the mixture into 6 crab croquettes. Chill the crab croquettes for 30 minutes until solid.
4. Place the flour, eggs, and breadcrumbs in three separate shallow dishes. Dust the crab croquettes in the flour, then dip them into the egg; lastly, roll the croquettes onto the breadcrumbs until they are well coated on all sides.
5. Brush the crab croquettes with the remaining 1 teaspoon of olive oil and cook them at 180°C/360°F for about 10 minutes, until they are cooked through. Bon appétit!

Creamy Sea Trout Salad

Air-fried Sea trout pairs perfectly with mayonnaise, yoghurt, and gherkins in this classic fish salad. Serve with avocado, cos lettuce, or air-roasted potatoes, if desired.

Preparation Time	Cooking Time	Servings
10 min + chilling time	11 min	2

Nutritional Information Per Serving

Energy value: 315 Kcal, Protein: 11.4g,
Carbohydrates: 31.4, Fats: 16.6

Ingredients

- 2 (about 150g each) sea trout fillets, skin-on, scaled
- 4 tbsp. mayonnaise
- 4 tbsp. natural yoghurt
- 1 tbsp small capers, rinsed
- 4 small gherkins, sliced
- 2 spring onions, finely sliced

Instructions

1. Pat the trout fillets dry using paper towels. Crush the peeled ginger and garlic using a garlic press.
2. Toss the trout fillets with the ginger-garlic mixture, followed by the other ingredients.
3. Cook the trout fillets at 195°C/390°degrees F for 5 minutes; turn the fillets over and cook for a further 6 minutes until opaque.
4. Break the fish into bite-sized strips and place in your fridge to cool completely. Toss the fish with the remaining ingredients.
5. Bon appétit!

Ginger Garlicky Cod Fish

Are you looking for a new, exciting way to cook cod fish? Try this recipe and thank me later!

Preparation Time	Cooking Time	Servings
5 min	10 min	3

Nutritional Information Per Serving

Energy value: 221 Kcal, Protein: 41.6g,
Carbohydrates: 4.3g, Fats: 2.9g

Ingredients

- 3 (about 160g each) cod fish fillets, skin-on
- 1 tsp. butter, at room temperature
- ½ tsp. garlic granules
- ½ tsp onion granules
- ¼ tsp. red pepper flakes
- ½ tsp. dried oregano
- Sea salt and ground black pepper, to your liking

Instructions

1. Pat the cod fish fillets dry using paper towels. Add the fish along with the remaining ingredients to a resealable bag; shake to coat well.
2. Arrange the fish fillets in the lightly-greased Air Fryer cooking basket.
3. Cook the fish fillets at 195°C/390°degrees F for 5 minutes; turn the fillets over and cook for a further 5 minutes, until opaque.
4. Bon appétit!

Scallop Salad

Skip the washing-up with this air-fried scallop dish! Scallops pair wonderfully with fresh lettuce, cabbage, and hard-boiled eggs.

Preparation Time	Cooking Time	Servings
5 min	7 min	4

Nutritional Information Per Serving

Energy value: 163 Kcal, Protein: 16.1g,
Carbohydrates: 14.7g, Fats: 4.7g

Ingredients

- 400g sea scallops, cleaned
- 2 tsp. extra-virgin olive oil
- Sea salt and ground black pepper, to taste
- 1 head of Romaine lettuce
- 200g red cabbage, shredded
- 1 medium lemon, freshly squeezed
- 1 tbsp. balsamic vinegar
- 1 hard-boiled egg, sliced

Instructions

1. Pat the scallops dry using paper towels. Toss the scallops with 1 teaspoon of olive oil, salt, and black pepper.
2. Cook the scallops at 200°C/395° F for 7 minutes, shaking the basket halfway through the cooking time. Careful not to overcook the scallops.
3. Peel the egg and cut it into slices; tear the lettuce into small pieces and add it to a salad bowl along with the shredded cabbage. Drizzle with lemon juice, balsamic vinegar, and the remaining 1 teaspoon of olive oil. Toss to combine.
4. Top your salad with the prepared scallops and eggs and enjoy!

Tilapia Fillets with Asparagus

Here is the recipe for the perfect crisp-skinned tilapia fillets with paprika and asparagus. This one-pot meal is all you need for a weeknight dinner with your beloved one.

Preparation Time	Cooking Time	Servings
5 min	19 min	2

Nutritional Information Per Serving

Energy value: 260 Kcal, Protein: 43.8g,
Carbohydrates: 6.4g, Fats: 6.3g

Ingredients

- 2 (about 160g each) cod fish fillets, skin-on
- 2 tsp. olive oil
- ½ tsp. garlic granules
- ¼ tsp. paprika
- Sea salt and ground black pepper, to your liking
- 200g asparagus tips

Instructions

1. Pat the tilapia fish fillets dry using paper towels. Toss the fish fillets with 1 teaspoon of olive oil, garlic, paprika, salt, and black pepper in the lightly-greased Air Fryer cooking basket.
2. Cook the fish fillets at180°C/360°F for about 13 minutes, turning them over halfway through the cooking time.
3. Toss asparagus tips with the remaining teaspoon of olive oil, salt, and black pepper.
4. Turn the temperature to 200°C/400°F, top fish fillets with asparagus, and continue cooking for 6 minutes more, until the fish is opaque, and the asparagus is crisp-tender.
5. Bon appétit!

Calamari Rings

If you are tired of greasy junk food, try these air-fried, marinated, and saucy calamari rings. It makes the perfect midweek meal for two!

Preparation Time	Cooking Time	Servings

5 min + 1 hr marinating	5 min	2

Nutritional Information Per Serving

Energy value: 419 Kcal, Protein: 33.4g,
Carbohydrates: 51.4g, Fats: 6.1g

Ingredients

- 300g squid, cleaned and cut into rings
- 100 ml stout
- 1 tbsp. brown mustard
- 60g all-purpose flour
- 1 small egg
- 60g (½ cup) breadcrumbs
- 1 teaspoon Cajun seasoning mix

Instructions

1. Pat the squid rings dry with paper towels. Add the squid, stout, and mustard to a ceramic bowl, cover, and let it marinate in your fridge for about 1 hour. Discard the marinade.
2. Place the flour in a shallow bowl. In another bowl, whisk the egg. Add the breadcrumbs and Cajun seasoning mix to a third shallow bowl.
3. Dust the calamari rings in the flour. Then, dip them into the egg mixture; finally, coat them with the breadcrumb mixture on all sides.
4. Lay the calamari rings in the Air Fryer cooking basket and cook them at 200°C/400°F for 5 minutes. Serve warm and enjoy!

Fish En Papillote

Do not be fooled by this fancy name. Fish En Papillote aka 'fish in pockets' are so simple to make in an Air Fryer! Air frying is the perfect method to cook those juicy, flaky snapper fillets with fork-tender vegetables.

Preparation Time	Cooking Time	Servings
5 min	15 min	2

Nutritional Information Per Serving

Energy value: 338 Kcal, Protein: 49.4g,
Carbohydrates: 22.1g Fats: 6g

Ingredients

- 2 (160g) snapper fillets, skin-on
- 1 shallot, peeled and cut into wedges
- 1 large carrot, trimmed and sliced
- 200g small broccoli florets
- 1 medium bell pepper, seeded and sliced
- 1 tsp. olive oil
- Sea salt and freshly ground black pepper, to taste
- 1 tsp. paprika
- 2 rosemary sprigs

Instructions

1. Pat the fish dry using paper towels. Tear off 2 squares of parchment.
2. Assemble the packets: Place the fish fillet in the centre of one side of the parchment paper. Top the fish with the other ingredients. Next, create a half-moon shape with the parchment paper, folding as you go and sealing the food inside.
3. Cook the fish en papillote at 195°C/390°F for about 15 minutes.
4. Bon appétit!

Shrimp Salad

You probably have a seafood salad recipe in your back pocket, but this air-fried shrimp salad may become your new go-to. It is incredibly fresh, crispy, and nutritious!

Preparation Time	Cooking Time	Servings
5 min	6 min	4

Nutritional Information Per Serving

Energy value: 173 Kcal, Protein: 31.2g,
Carbohydrates: 5.7g, Fats: 3.3g

Ingredients

- 600g shrimp, peeled and deveined
- 2 tsp. extra-virgin olive oil
- 1 tbsp. Old Bay seasoning
- Sea salt and ground black pepper, to taste
- 2 handfuls mixed greens
- 1 medium cucumber, sliced
- 1 medium carrot, grated
- 1 medium lemon, freshly squeezed

Instructions

1. Toss your shrimp with 1 teaspoon of olive oil and spices.
2. Air fry your shrimp at 200°C/395° F for 6 minutes, shaking the basket halfway through the cooking time.
3. Toss your shrimp with the remaining ingredients and enjoy!

Tuna with Horseradish Sauce

Many studies have proven that eating tuna is associated with a reduced risk of cardiovascular disease. But did you know it can also improve your immune system and reduce depression?

Preparation Time	Cooking Time	Servings
5 min	14 min	3

Nutritional Information Per Serving

Energy value: 38 Kcal, Protein: 32.7g,
Carbohydrates: 1.4, Fats: 18.1

Ingredients

- 400g tuna steaks, 2cm thick
- 1tsp. olive oil
- 40g mayonnaise
- 40 ml plain yogurt
- 1 spring onion, chopped
- 1 tbsp. horseradish

Instructions

1. Pat the tuna steaks dry with paper towels and brush them with olive oil. Transfer the tuna steaks to the lightly-greased cooking basket.
2. Cook the tuna steaks at 200°C/395° F for 7 minutes; turn the tuna steaks over and cook them for a further 6-7 minutes.
3. In the meantime, whisk the remaining ingredients to make the horseradish sauce and on the tuna steaks once it's ready.
4. Bon appétit!

Salmon Fish Cakes

Although you can cook fish cakes in a frying pan, everything becomes healthier in the Air Fryer. You will need only 2 teaspoons of a good-quality oil and a pinch of imagination!

Preparation Time	Cooking Time	Servings
5 min	22 min	3

Nutritional Information Per Serving

Energy value: 413 Kcal, Protein: 32.7g,
Carbohydrates: 41g, Fats: 12.4g

Ingredients

- 350g salmon fillets
- 1 tsp. cayenne pepper
- Sea salt and ground black pepper, to taste
- 2 tsp. olive oil
- 200g cooked potatoes, mashed
- 1 tsp. yellow mustard
- ½ tsp. fresh ginger, peeled and minced
- 1 large garlic clove, minced
- 1 tbsp. parsley, minced
- 3 tbsp. plain flour
- 1 egg, beaten
- 100g dried breadcrumbs

Instructions

1. Pat the salmon fillets dry using paper towels. Toss salmon fillets with cayenne pepper, salt, black pepper, and 1 teaspoon of olive oil.
2. Cook salmon fillets at 200°C/400°degrees F for 6 minutes; turn the fillets over and cook for a further 5-6 minutes; after that, break the fish into large flakes.
3. Thoroughly combine the potatoes, mustard, ginger, garlic, parsley, flour, and egg; fold in the fish and gently stir to combine. Shape the mixture into patties.
4. Tip the breadcrumbs onto a plate, and roll the patties onto the breadcrumbs until they are well coated on all sides.
5. Place the patties in the lightly-greased cooking basket. Brush fish cakes with the remaining olive oil. Air fry the fish cakes at 180°C/360°F for about 10 minutes, until they are cooked through. Enjoy!

CHAPTER 5 SIDE DISHES & APPETIZERS

Don't Forget To Download Your Bonus PDF With The Colored Images

STEP BY STEP Guide To Access-

1. Open Your Phones (Or Any Device You Want The Book On) Back Camera. The Back Camera Is The One You use as if you are taking a picture of someone.
2. Simply point your Camera at the QR code and 'tap' the QR code with your finger to focus the camera.
3. A link / pop up will appear. Simply tap that (and make sure you have internet connection) and the FREE PDF containing all of the colored images should appear.
4. If You Click On The File And It Says 'The File Is Too Big To Preview' Simply click 'Download' and it will download the full book onto your phone!
5. Now you have access to these FOREVER. Simply 'Bookmark' The tab it opened on, or download the document and take wherever you want.
6. Repeat this on any device you want it on!

Any Issues / Feedback/ Troubleshooting please email: anthonypublishing123@gmail.com and our customer service team will help you! We want to make sure you have the BEST experience with our books!

Herb Roast Potatoes

If you want to save lots of oven room during holidays and family gatherings, you can cook roasted potatoes in your Air Fryer. The recipe calls for rosemary and oregano, but feel free to use your favourite spice mix!

Preparation Time	Cooking Time	Servings
5 min	22 min	4

Nutritional Information Per Serving

Energy value: 113 Kcal, Protein: 2.8g,
Carbohydrates: 23.2g, Fats: 1.2g

Ingredients

- 500g Maris Piper potatoes, peeled
- 1 tsp. olive oil
- Sea salt and ground black pepper, to taste
- 1 tsp. dried rosemary
- 1 tsp. dried oregano

Instructions

1. Cut the potatoes into quarters and toss them with olive oil, salt, and pepper.
2. Place the potatoes in the Air Fryer cooking basket and cook them at 190°C/380°F for about 10 minutes; shake the basket and continue cooking for 10 to 12 minutes more, until they are cooked through and slightly charred.
3. Once cooked, toss in the rosemary and oregano. Serve immediately and enjoy!

Courgette Fritters

Pro tip –squeeze out as much moisture as you can from the grated courgettes; otherwise, the liquid will spoil the batter. Add chilli flakes if you prefer spicy fritters.

Preparation Time	Cooking Time	Servings
15 min	20 min	3

Nutritional Information Per Serving

Energy value: 146 Kcal, Protein: 7.1g,
Carbohydrates: 17.7, Fats: 5.3g

Ingredients

- 100g courgette, grated
- 50g plain flour
- 1 large egg, beaten
- 1 scallion stalk, chopped
- Zest of 1 lemon
- 20g Parmesan cheese, preferably freshly grated
- A pinch of chilli flakes (optional)
- ¼ tsp. dried dill (optional)
- Sea salt and ground black pepper, to taste
- 1 tsp. olive oil

Instructions

1. Toss the courgette with ½ teaspoon of sea salt in a colander; let it sit for about 15 minutes; after that, squeeze out all excess moisture using a paper towel.
2. Thoroughly combine the grated courgettes with the remaining ingredients. Shape the mixture into small patties and arrange them in the lightly-greased cooking basket.
3. Air-fry the courgette fritters at 200°C/395°F for about 20 minutes, until they are thoroughly cooked.
4. Bon appétit!

Traditional Ratatouille

This traditional French Provençal dish is a cinch to make in the Air Fryer. This chunky vegetable stew with fragrant herbs may become your next family favourite.

Preparation Time

5 min

Cooking Time

15 min

Servings

4

Nutritional Information Per Serving

Energy value: 111 Kcal, Protein: 3.7g,
Carbohydrates: 20.gj, Fats: 3g

Ingredients

- 1 medium aubergine, sliced
- 1 medium courgette, sliced
- 2 garlic cloves, chopped
- 1 medium onion, sliced
- 2 medium tomatoes, diced
- 2 bell peppers, seeded and sliced
- 2 tsp. olive oil
- 1 tbsp. herb de Provence
- Sea salt and ground black pepper, to taste
- 200ml tomato sauce

Instructions

1. Begin by preheating your Air Fryer to 200°C/395°F.
2. Toss the vegetables with olive oil and spices. Arrange the vegetables in an alternating pattern in a lightly-greased baking tin. Spoon the tomato sauce over the vegetables.
3. Bake your ratatouille in the preheated Air Fryer for about 15 minutes, until cooked through.
4. Bon appétit!

Butter Cabbage

Cabbage is a nutrient-rich vegetable with numerous health benefits, from reduced blood pressure to the decreased risk of serious heart disease. If you do not like raw cabbage, use air frying and short cooking time to preserve its nutrients.

Preparation Time

5 min

Cooking Time

15 min

Servings

4

Nutritional Information Per Serving

Energy value: 102 Kcal, Protein: 2.4g,
Carbohydrates: 12.2g, Fats: 6.3g

Ingredients

- 1 green cabbage head, cleaned
- 2 tbsp. butter, melted
- 1 garlic clove, minced
- Sea salt and ground black pepper, to taste
- 1 tsp. hot paprika
- 1 tsp. lemon zest, grated

Instructions

1. Begin by preheating your Air Fryer to 195°C/380°F. Cut the cabbage into wedges.
2. Toss the cabbage wedges with the other ingredients and transfer them to the lightly-greased cooking basket.
3. Air fry the cabbage wedges for about 15 minutes, until they are crisp on the outside and tender on the inside.
4. Enjoy!

Tofu with Vegetables

It's time for a vegan recipe! Packed with tofu, vegs, and, spices, this air-fried side dish may become your new go-to weeknight winner.

Preparation Time	Cooking Time	Servings
5 min	12 min	4

Nutritional Information Per Serving

Energy value: 214 Kcal, Protein: 19.7g,
Carbohydrates: 14.4g, Fats: 10.7g

Ingredients

- 400g tofu, pressed & cut into bite-sized cubes
- 1 bell pepper, seeded and diced
- 1 medium onion, diced
- 100ml tomato sauce
- 400g courgettes, diced
- ½ tsp. garlic granules
- 1 tsp. soy sauce
- 1 tsp. olive oil

Instructions

1. Toss the ingredients in a baking tin until everything is well coated with spices.
2. Lower the baking tin into the Air Fryer cooking basket.
3. Bake the tofu and vegetables at 200°C/395°F for 12 minutes, until cooked through.
4. Bon appétit!

Beet and Avocado Salad

Beets are low in calories but high in nutrients. This superfood supports your brain health as well as help fight inflammation. Avocado is packed with beta-carotene and healthy, beneficial fats.

Preparation Time	Cooking Time	Servings
5 min	40 min	4

Nutritional Information Per Serving

Energy value: 177 Kcal, Protein: 18.7g,
Carbohydrates: 14.5g, Fats: 11g

Ingredients

- 500g red beets, peeled
- 1 tbsp. extra-virgin olive oil
- 1 tbsp. apple cider vinegar
- 1 tbsp. lemon juice, preferably freshly squeezed
- 1 tsp. hot mustard
- 1 garlic clove, minced
- ¼ tsp. cumin, ground
- Sea salt and ground black pepper, to taste
- ½ small bunch parsley, roughly chopped
- 1 medium avocado

Instructions

1. Place the beets in a single layer in the lightly-greased Air Fryer cooking basket.
2. Cook the beets at 200°C/395°F for 40 minutes, shaking the basket halfway through the cooking time.
3. In the meantime, place the avocado halves on a cutting board, whack the pit with the sharp end of the knife to remove it easily and cut your avocado into slices.
4. Let the beets cool and cut them into slices; then, toss in the remaining olive oil, vinegar, lemon juice, mustard, garlic, and spices.
5. Place the salad in the fridge until ready to serve. Garnish the beet salad with parsley and the avocado.
6. Enjoy!

Griddled Aubergine Rounds

Charred and topped with cheese, these aubergine rounds make a great addition to your festive platter. You can serve aubergine rounds as an alongside meze or with your soup.

Preparation Time  5 min

Cooking Time 15 min

Servings 4

Nutritional Information Per Serving

Energy value: 190 Kcal, Protein: 10.1g,
Carbohydrates: 21.1g, Fats: 8.7g

Ingredients

- 2 medium aubergines
- 1 tsp. olive oil
- 2 oregano sprigs, leaves picked and finely chopped
- Sea salt and ground black pepper, to your liking
- ¼ tsp. sumac
- 100g Parmesan cheese, grated
- 1 tbsp. fresh parsley, chopped

Instructions

1. Cut aubergines into 1cm-thick slices and toss them with olive oil, oregano, salt, black pepper, and sumac. Arrange them on the lightly-greased Air Fryer cooking basket.
2. Cook the aubergine rounds at 200°C/395°F for about 10 minutes; cook the aubergine rounds in batches.
3. Top the aubergine rounds with cheese; continue to cook for 5 more until the aubergine is completely soft throughout and the cheese has melted.
4. Garnish aubergine rounds with the fresh parsley and enjoy!

Butter Garlic Asparagus

Asparagus is an excellent source of vitamin A, vitamin C, riboflavin, and folate. Looking to consume more asparagus? Keep reading the recipe below!

Preparation Time 5 min

Cooking Time 7 min

Servings 4

Nutritional Information Per Serving

Energy value: 84 Kcal, Protein: 3.1g,
Carbohydrates: 6.5, Fats: 6g

Ingredients

- 500g asparagus spears, trimmed
- 2 tbsp. butter, melted
- 1 garlic clove, minced
- 1 tsp. cayenne pepper
- A handful dill, chopped (optional)
- Sea salt and ground black pepper, to taste
- 1 tsp. lemon zest, grated

Instructions

1. Begin by preheating your Air Fryer to 200°C/400°F.
2. Toss the asparagus spears with the other ingredients and transfer them to the lightly-greased cooking basket.
3. Air fry the asparagus for about 7 minutes, until crisp-tender. Serve with some extra butter, if desired.
4. Enjoy!

Pigs-in-Blankets

If you do not have mini cocktail sausages on hand, you can cut large sausages into three to four pieces; just make sure that each piece of sausage is wrapped in one rasher of bacon. Since the bacon and sausages have a good amount of fat, you won't need any oil!

Preparation Time	Cooking Time	Servings
5 min	15 min	5

Nutritional Information Per Serving

Energy value: 363 Kcal, Protein: 13.1g,
Carbohydrates: 0.7g, Fats: 34.3

Ingredients
- 9 cocktail sausages
- 9 pancetta rashers
- Sea salt and ground black pepper, to taste

Instructions
1. Wrap your sausages in the pancetta slices and arrange them in the Air Frye cooking basket.
2. Cook pigs in the blanket at 180°C/360°F for about 15 minutes, until they are cooked through, and the pancetta is crisp.
3. Afterwards, sprinkle with salt and pepper and serve.
4. Bon appétit!

Okra Chips

Okra is a nutrient-rich food with numerous health benefits. It's rich in vitamins C, K1, and A, fibre, magnesium, and folate. Okra also contains antioxidants, which may have anticancer properties.

Preparation Time	Cooking Time	Servings
5 min	20 min	4

Nutritional Information Per Serving

Energy value: 98 Kcal, Protein: 3.1g,
Carbohydrates: 19.3g, Fats: 1.6g

Ingredients
- 500g okra, cleaned and trimmed
- 1 tsp. extra-virgin olive oil
- 50g cornmeal
- ½ tsp. ground coriander
- ½ tsp. turmeric powder
- Sea salt and ground black pepper, to taste

Instructions
1. Cut okra into halves lengthwise. Toss the okra halves with th other ingredients until they are well coated on all sides.
2. Cook your okra in the preheated Air Fryer at 180°C/360°F fc about 20 minutes, shaking the basket once or twice to ensur even cooking.
3. Bon appétit!

Mozzarella Sticks

Make your own cheese sticks featuring mozzarella coated in the most popular breading mix with flour, eggs, and breadcrumbs. The secret ingredient is Cajun seasoning.

Preparation Time	Cooking Time	Servings
5 min	6 min	4

Nutritional Information Per Serving

Energy value: 510 Kcal, Protein: 15.5g,
Carbohydrates: 57.4, Fats: 25.8

Ingredients

- 250g block firm mozzarella cheese
- 50g all-purpose flour
- 1 medium egg
- 100g breadcrumbs
- 1 tsp. Cajun seasoning
- 1 tsp. olive oil

Instructions

1. Cut your mozzarella into 1cm-thick finger-length strips. Next, set up your breading station. Place all-purpose flour in a shallow dish. In a separate dish, whisk the egg and mix the breadcrumbs with Cajun seasoning in a third dish.
   Start by dredging mozzarella sticks in the flour; then, dip them into the egg. Press mozzarella sticks into the breadcrumb mixture. Brush breaded mozzarella sticks with olive oil.
   Cook mozzarella sticks at 190°C/375°F for about 6 minutes.
   Serve with a spicy tomato sauce for even more delicious results. Bon appétit!

Sweet Potato Chips

Ready in under 35 minutes, sweet potato chips are the perfect savoury family snack. As a good alternative to classic potato chips, air-fried sweet potato chips are vibrant, healthy, and delicious.

Preparation Time	Cooking Time	Servings
25 min	15 min	4

Nutritional Information Per Serving

Energy value: 325 Kcal, Protein: 13.9g,
Carbohydrates: 14.9, Fats: 22.8

Ingredients

- 500g sweet potatoes, peeled
- 1 tsp. olive oil
- ½ tsp. garlic granules
- ½ tsp. onion granules
- Coarse sea salt and freshly ground black pepper, to taste
- 1 tsp. paprika

Instructions

1. Cut sweet potatoes into ½-cm thick slices. Place the sweet potato slices in a bowl of cold water; let them sit for about 20 minutes.
2. Toss sweet potato slices with the remaining ingredients. Cook sweet potato chips in the preheated Air Fryer at 180°C/360°F for about 7 minutes; shake the cooking basket and cook for a further 7 to 8 minutes until golden and crispy.
3. Serve sweet potato chips with a sauce for dipping, if desired. Enjoy!

Broccoli with Bacon

Spicy Stuffed Mushrooms

What's better than air-fried broccoli florets coated with mayo and spices? Broccoli bites with bacon! Serve as a side dish or a stellar addition to a mezze platter.

Stuffed mushrooms are a popular appetizer worldwide. This time, we added peppers to spice them up and take this air-fried dish to the next level!

Preparation Time	Cooking Time	Servings

5 min	7 min	4

Preparation Time	Cooking Time	Servings
5 min	10 min	4

Nutritional Information Per Serving

Energy value: 192 Kcal, Protein: 6.9g,
Carbohydrates: 9.7g, Fats: 14.9g

Nutritional Information Per Serving

Energy value: 102 Kcal, Protein: 4.5g,
Carbohydrates: 4.5g, Fats: 7.9g

Ingredients
- 500g broccoli florets
- 25g mayonnaise
- ½ tsp. dried oregano
- ½ tsp. dried basil
- Sea salt and ground black pepper, to your liking
- 100g bacon rashers

Ingredients
- 1 tbsp. olive oil
- Sea salt and ground black pepper, to your liking
- ½ tsp. dried rosemary
- ½ tsp. red pepper flakes
- 1 yellow bell pepper, seeded and chopped
- 1 red chilli pepper, seeded and chopped
- 50g cheddar cheese, preferably freshly grated

Instructions
1. Cover the broccoli florets with mayonnaise, oregano, basil, salt, and black pepper. Arrange them in the lightly-greased Air Fryer cooking basket and top with the bacon rashers.
2. Cook the broccoli and bacon at 200°C/395°F for 6 to 7 minutes, shaking the basket once or twice during the cooking time.
3. Bon appétit!

Instructions
1. Remove the stems from the mushroom caps; chop the stems and save for later.
2. In a mixing bowl, thoroughly combine the remaining ingredients, including the reserved mushroom stems; divide the filling among the mushroom caps and top with the cheese.
3. Cook the stuffed mushrooms in the preheated Air Fryer at 190°C/375°F for about 10 minutes.
4. Bon appétit!

Roasted Vegetables

A perfect side for all kinds of main dishes, or simply delicious with a dollop of a mayo sauce or soured cream.

Preparation Time	Cooking Time	Servings
5 min	15 min	4

Nutritional Information Per Serving

Energy value: 94 Kcal, Protein: 4.5g,
Carbohydrates: 16.6g, Fats: 2.3g

Ingredients

- 2 large carrots, cut into long sticks
- 1 medium courgette, cut into rounds
- 1 large red onion, sliced
- 2 bell peppers, seeded and halved
- 1 tsp. olive oil
- ½ tsp. cayenne pepper
- ½ tsp. garlic granules
- Kosher salt and ground black pepper, to taste

Instructions

1. Toss your vegetables with olive oil and spices. Preheat your Air Fryer to 190°C/375°F.
2. Cook the carrots and courgette in the Air Fryer cooking basket for approximately 8 minutes.
3. Add the onion and peppers last, and continue to cook for 7 minutes more, until cooked through.
4. Bon appétit!

Roasted Butternut Squash Mash

You can add some extra herbs and butter before serving. Keep leftover butternut squash mash in an airtight container in your fridge for up to 4 days.

Preparation Time	Cooking Time	Servings
5 min	20 min	4

Nutritional Information Per Serving

Energy value: 84 Kcal, Protein: 1.4g,
Carbohydrates: 15.1g, Fats: 3g

Ingredients

- 500g butternut squash, peeled
- 1 tbsp. butter, unsalted
- ½ tsp. ground cinnamon
- 1 tsp. garlic granules
- 1 tbsp. parsley leaves, roughly chopped

Instructions

1. Start by preheating your Air Fryer to 195°C/390°F. Cut the butternut squash into small wedges. Toss the butternut squash with the butter, cinnamon, and garlic granules.
2. Roast the butternut squash in the preheated Air Fryer for 10 minutes. Shake the basket and continue to cook for 10 minutes more.
3. Purée the butternut squash using an immersion blender or potato masher. Garnish butternut squash mash with fresh parsley leaves.
4. Bon appétit!

Classic Potato Latkes

You can use Maris Piper potatoes for this recipe; other good additions include cheese, zucchini, parsley, and mushrooms.

Preparation Time	Cooking Time	Servings
5 min	25 min	4

Nutritional Information Per Serving

Energy value: 211 Kcal, Protein: 7.6g,
Carbohydrates: 40g, Fats: 2.4g

Ingredients

- 2 large potatoes, scrubbed, unpeeled
- 1 small onion, peeled and chopped
- 2 medium eggs, beaten
- 4 tbsp. plain flour
- 1 tbsp. sage
- 1 tbsp. rosemary
- Sea salt and ground black pepper, to taste
- ¼ tsp. cayenne pepper

Instructions

1. Coarsely grate your potatoes and wring out the liquids with a clean tea towel.
2. Add the rest of the ingredients to the grated potatoes. Brush the bottom of the Air Fryer cooking basket with non-stick cooking oil.
3. Shape the mixture into latkes, flattening gently with a spatula.
4. Cook your latkes at 195°C/395°F for about 13 minutes. Turn them over and cook for a further 12 minutes, until thoroughly cooked.
5. Bon appétit!

Corn on the Cob

Liven up corn on the cob with the garlic butter and cilantro to make a vibrant side dish. Serve with your favourite air-fried sausages or fish fillets.

Preparation Time	Cooking Time	Servings
5 min	10 min	2

Nutritional Information Per Serving

Energy value: 268 Kcal, Protein: 4.4g,
Carbohydrates: 30g, Fats: 17.1g

Ingredients

- 40g butter, softened
- 1 garlic clove, crushed
- 2 ears corn on the cob, halved
- 1 tbsp. fresh cilantro leaves, minced

Instructions

1. Mix the butter and garlic in a small bowl. Cut 4 pieces of tin foil and place ½ of the cob on each piece. Next, top them with the garlic butter and seal the edges to form the packets.
2. Transfer the packets to the cooking basket. Bake corn on the cob at 200°C/400°F for about 5 minutes; turn them over and continue to cook for 5 minutes more until tender.
3. Garnish the corn on the cob with fresh cilantro leaves.
4. Bon appétit!

Fennel with Cherry Tomatoes

This recipe is endlessly customizable. You can add onions, peppers, or pumpkin seeds. If you do not have goat cheese on hand, you can use feta or blue cheese. The possibilities are endless!

Preparation Time	Cooking Time	Servings

5 min	10 min	2

Nutritional Information Per Serving

Energy value: 168 Kcal, Protein: 9.5g,
Carbohydrates: 11.5g, Fats: 10.1g

Ingredients

- 1 medium bulb fennel, sliced
- 1 tsp. lemon juice, preferably freshly squeezed
- 1 tbsp. extra-virgin olive oil
- Sea salt and ground black pepper, to taste
- 1 tbsp. fresh parsley leaves, chopped
- 50g goat cheese, crumbled

Instructions

1. Cut off the fennel top and discard the outer layers; then, cut the fennel into slices.
2. Toss the fennel slices with lemon juice, olive oil, salt, and black pepper.
3. Transfer the fennel slices and cherry tomatoes to the lightly-greased Air Fryer cooking basket.
4. Roast the fennel slices and cherry tomatoes in the preheated Air Fryer at 180°C/360°F for about 8 minutes.
5. Shake the cooking basket and continue to cook for a further 7 minutes, until your fennel is crisp-tender and slightly charred.
6. Garnish your vegetables with fresh parsley and cheese. Enjoy!

Carrots with Leek and Tomatoes

Try these amazing air-roasted sticky carrots with leeks and cherry tomatoes. The secret to this addictive side dish is maple syrup and dried dill.

Preparation Time	Cooking Time	Servings
5 min	15 min	4

Nutritional Information Per Serving

Energy value: 118 Kcal, Protein: 1.9g,
Carbohydrates: 20.4g, Fats: 3.9g

Ingredients

- 500g carrots
- 1 medium leek
- 200g cherry tomatoes
- 1 tbsp. avocado oil (or canola oil)
- 1 tbsp. maple syrup
- ¼ teaspoon dried dill
- Kosher salt and red pepper, to your liking

Instructions

1. Cut the leek and carrots in half, and then, cut them into quarters lengthwise. Toss the leek, carrots, and cherry tomatoes with the other ingredients.
2. Place your vegetables in the lightly-greased Air Fryer cooking basket. Cook the vegetables at 180°C/360°F for about 15 minutes, shaking the basket halfway through the cooking time to ensure even cooking.
3. Place warm vegetables on a serving platter and serve immediately. Enjoy!

Vegetarian Stuffed Peppers

Learn how to make vegetarian stuffed peppers in your Air Fryer and delight your taste buds. These peppers are filled with canned beans, brown mushrooms, and grated Parmesan cheese fried to perfection.

Preparation Time	Cooking Time	Servings
5 min	15 min	4

Nutritional Information Per Serving

Energy value: 155 Kcal, Protein: 8.5g,
Carbohydrates: 23.1g, Fats: 4.6g

Ingredients

- 4 bell peppers
- 1 tsp. olive oil
- 100g canned or boiled pinto beans, rinsed, and drained
- Sea salt and ground black pepper, to taste
- ¼ tsp. cayenne pepper
- ½ tsp. ground cumin
- 40g Parmesan cheese, grated
- 200g brown mushrooms, chopped

Instructions

1. Remove the tops and seeds from the peppers. Brush the peppers with olive oil. Mash the beans with a fork; then, add the other ingredients and mix to combine.
2. Fill the peppers with the prepared stuffing. Arrange the stuffed peppers in a lightly-greased Air Fryer cooking basket.
3. Air-fry the stuffed peppers at 200°C/400°F for about 15 minutes, until cooked through.
4. Bon appétit!

Szechuan Green Beans

This is a simple recipe for Szechuan-style air-fried green beans you can prepare in less than 15 minutes! Green beans pair wonderfully with brown rice, roast pork, and smoked salmon.

Preparation Time	Cooking Time	Servings
5 min	7 min	4

Nutritional Information Per Serving

Energy value: 84 Kcal, Protein: 2.7g,
Carbohydrates: 10.1g, Fats: 4.4g

Ingredients

- 500g green beans, cleaned and trimmed
- 1 tbsp. olive oil
- 1 fresh garlic, peeled and pressed
- ½ tsp. fresh ginger, peeled and pressed
- ½ tsp. cayenne pepper
- 1 tbsp. soy sauce
- 1 tsp. Szechuan peppercorns, crushed

Instructions

1. In a large mixing bowl, toss green beans with the remaining ingredients.
2. Air-fry the green beans at 200°C/400°F for about 7 minutes until they start to blister. Make sure to shake the basket halfway through the cooking time to ensure even cooking.
3. Bon appétit!

CHAPTER 6
VEGAN

**Don't Forget To Download Your Bonus PDF With
The Colored Images**

STEP BY STEP Guide To Access-

1. Open Your Phones (Or Any Device You Want The Book On) Back Camera. The Back Camera Is The One You use as if you are taking a picture of someone.
2. Simply point your Camera at the QR code and 'tap' the QR code with your finger to focus the camera.
3. A link / pop up will appear. Simply tap that (and make sure you have internet connection) and the FREE PDF containing all of the colored images should appear.
4. If You Click On The File And It Says 'The File Is Too Big To Preview' Simply click 'Download' and it will download the full book onto your phone!
5. Now you have access to these FOREVER. Simply 'Bookmark' The tab it opened on, or download the document and take wherever you want.
6. Repeat this on any device you want it on!

Any Issues / Feedback/ Troubleshooting please email: anthonypublishing123@gmail.com and our customer service team will help you! We want to make sure you have the BEST experience with our books!

Aubergine Burger

These vegan burgers are loaded with vegetables, hummus, and tofu mayonnaise. Other good topping ideas include fresh lettuce, tomatoes, or roasted peppers from a jar. For a healthier version of these burgers, use multi-seed bread rolls.

Preparation Time	Cooking Time	Servings
5 min	**20 min**	**4**

Nutritional Information Per Serving

Energy value: 286 Kcal, Protein: 7.7g,
Carbohydrates: 39.3g, Fats: 11.4g

Ingredients

- 1 small aubergine, wide middle section cut into 4 rounds
- 1 tbsp. olive oil
- 2 tsp. harissa
- ½ tsp. ground cumin
- ½ tsp. ground coriander
- Sea salt and ground black pepper, to taste
- 2 tbsp. cornmeal
- 4 ciabatta rolls, halved
- 4 tbsp. hummus
- 4 tbsp. tofu mayonnaise
- 1 small onions, sliced

Instructions

1. Toss the aubergine rounds with olive oil, harissa, cumin, coriander, salt, black pepper, and cornmeal. Toss until they are well coated.
2. Roast the aubergine rounds at 200°C/395°F for about 15 minutes. After that, toast ciabatta rolls at 160°C/320°F for about 4 minutes.
3. Lastly, spread the rolls with hummus and tofu mayonnaise. Place your aubergine rounds and onion slices on top. Serve immediately and enjoy!

Stuffed Winter Squash

Winter squash is a great source of vitamin A & vitamin C, fibre, and numerous essential minerals. It may boost your immune system and lower your risk of certain types of cancer.

Preparation Time	Cooking Time	Servings
5 min	**35 min**	**4**

Nutritional Information Per Serving

Energy value: 246 Kcal, Protein: 3.8g,
Carbohydrates: 15.7g, Fats: 21.1g

Ingredients

- 500g winter squash, unpeeled
- 1 tsp. coconut oil
- 1 tsp. pumpkin spice mix
- Sea salt and ground black pepper, to taste
- 200g vegan coconut cream
- 100g black olives, pitted and sliced
- 8 cherry tomatoes, quartered

Instructions

1. Cut the winter squash into wedges and brush them wit coconut oil; season with spices.
2. Place the winter squash wedges in the lightly-greased Air Frye cooking basket.
3. Bake the winter squash wedges at 180°C/360°F for about 3 minutes.
4. Top the winter squash with vegan coconut cream, black olive and tomatoes.
5. Bon appétit!

Tempeh Salad

Tempeh is a star of many vegetarian and vegan dishes. Flavour your tempeh with soy sauce, red pepper, and BBQ sauce for a delicious result!

Preparation Time	Cooking Time	Servings
5 min	10 min	4

Nutritional Information Per Serving

Energy value: 34 Kcal, Protein: 24.3g,
Carbohydrates: 18.5g, Fats: 17.1g

Ingredients

- 500g tempeh, pressed and cubed
- 1 tsp. soy sauce
- ½ tsp. red pepper flakes, crushed
- 30 ml BBQ sauce
- 1 bell peppers, seeded and cut into strips
- 1 large carrots, chopped
- 2 handfuls Romaine lettuce, shredded
- 1 small onion, thinly sliced
- 1 tbsp. extra-virgin olive oil
- 1 tbsp. apple cider vinegar

Instructions

1. Cut your tempeh into bite-sized cubes and toss them with soy sauce, red pepper flakes, and BBQ sauce.
2. Cook your tempeh at 190°C/380°F for about 10 minutes; turn them over and cook for a further 5 minutes.
3. Toss the tempeh cubes with the remaining ingredients and serve immediately.
4. Bon appétit!

Vegan Tacos

Who doesn't love tacos? You can swap potatoes for cauliflower and add your favourite toppings for delicious meat-free tacos in this top-tier air-frier recipe.

Preparation Time	Cooking Time	Servings
10 min	25 min	2

Nutritional Information Per Serving

Energy value: 325 Kcal, Protein: 13.9g,
Carbohydrates: 14.9, Fats: 22.8

Ingredients

- 400g potatoes
- 1 bell pepper, seeded and sliced
- 1 tsp. olive oil
- Sea salt and ground black pepper, to your liking
- 1 tsp. cayenne pepper
- ½ tsp. dried oregano
- 2 whole-meal tortilla wraps
- 2 tbsp. hummus
- 1 tsp. Dijon mustard
- 1 handful lettuce, shredded
- 1 small ripe tomato, halved (you may also use ketchup)

Instructions

1. Peel the potatoes and cut them into bite-sized chunks. Toss the potatoes and peppers with olive oil, salt, black pepper, cayenne pepper, and oregano
2. Place the potatoes in the Air Fryer cooking basket and cook them at 190°C/380°F for about 10 minutes; shake the basket, add peppers, and continue cooking for 15 minutes longer, until the vegetables are cooked through and appear slightly charred.
3. Spread the hummus and mustard on the tortilla wraps, laying lettuce and tomato slices on top. Divide the roasted vegetables between warm tortillas.
4. Serve immediately and enjoy!

Tofu-Stuffed Mushrooms

Try these air-fried Portobella mushrooms topped with tofu, peppers, and herbs. Ready in about 15 minutes, they are easy to make and fun to eat!

Preparation Time	Cooking Time	Servings
5 min	10 min	2

Nutritional Information Per Serving

Energy value: 222 Kcal, Protein: 13.8g,
Carbohydrates: 21.5g, Fats: 12.2g

Ingredients

- 4 large Portobella mushrooms
- 100g firm tofu, crumbled
- 1 tbsp. olive oil
- Sea salt and ground black pepper, to your liking
- ½ tsp. dried rosemary
- ½ tsp. dried basil
- 1 yellow bell pepper, seeded and chopped
- 1 red chili pepper, seeded and chopped

Instructions

1. Remove the stems from the mushroom caps; chop the stems and save for later.
2. In a mixing bowl, thoroughly combine the remaining ingredients, including the reserved mushroom stems; divide the filling among the mushroom caps.
3. Cook the stuffed mushrooms in the preheated Air Fryer at 190°C/375°F for about 10 minutes.
4. Bon appétit!

Vegan French Toast

You can't go wrong with this egg-free and dairy-free vegan breakfast! You can substitute soy milk with any type of unsweetened dairy-free milk.

Preparation Time	Cooking Time	Servings
5 min	15 min	2

Nutritional Information Per Serving

Energy value: 227 Kcal, Protein: 4.7g,
Carbohydrates: 36.3,g Fats: 7.1g

Ingredients

- 4 thick slices of ciabatta bread
- 50ml soy milk
- 20g corn starch
- ¼ tsp. turmeric powder
- 1 tsp. ground flaxseed meal
- ½ tsp. baking powder
- ½ tsp. ground cinnamon
- 2 tsp. coconut oil, room temperature
- 2 tsp. pure maple syrup

Instructions

1. Begin by preheating your Air Fryer to 180°C/360°F.
2. In a mixing bowl, whisk the soy milk, corn starch, flaxseed mea baking powder, and cinnamon.
3. Dip bread slices in the custard mixture until they are well coate on all sides. Brush them with coconut oil.
4. Cook French toast in the preheated Air Fryer for about 1 minutes, turning halfway through the cooking time to ensur even cooking.
5. Serve French toast with maple syrup and enjoy!

Stuffed Aubergine Rolls

Try these healthy vegetable rolls filled with chickpeas and roasted peppers for an easy, healthy, and filling midweek meal. Serve with zesty lime wedges and vegan mayonnaise.

Preparation Time	Cooking Time	Servings
5 min	10 min	2

Nutritional Information Per Serving

Energy value: 185 Kcal, Protein: 7.3g,
Carbohydrates: 32.9g, Fats: 4.4g

Ingredients

- 1 medium aubergine
- 1 tsp. olive oil
- 100g canned or boiled chickpeas, rinsed and drained
- 100g roasted peppers in a jar, chopped
- Sea salt and ground black pepper, to taste
- ¼ tsp. cayenne pepper
- ½ tsp. ground cumin

Instructions

1. Cut aubergines lengthwise into ½cm-thick slices and toss them with olive oil. Arrange them on the lightly-greased Air Fryer cooking basket.
2. Cook the aubergine slices at 200°C/395°F for about 10 minutes; cook the aubergine slices in batches.
3. Meanwhile, mash canned chickpeas with roasted peppers, salt, black pepper, cayenne pepper, and ground cumin.
4. Top the aubergine slices with the chickpea mixture; roll them up and serve warm.
5. Enjoy!

Traditional Falafel

Air frying is one of the best ways to cook a healthy and delicious falafel. Serve warm falafel balls in pita sandwiches with tahini sauce and fresh salad.

Preparation Time	Cooking Time	Servings
5 min	20 min	3

Nutritional Information Per Serving

Energy value: 22 Kcal, Protein: 8.3g,
Carbohydrates: 30.9g, Fats: 7.1g

Ingredients

- 100g dried chickpeas, soaked overnight
- 30g breadcrumbs
- ½ tsp. baking soda
- 1 small onion, peeled and diced
- 1 large garlic clove
- 1 small bunch parsley
- Sea salt and freshly ground black pepper, to taste
- 1 tbsp. olive oil

Instructions

1. Add all the ingredients to a bowl of your food processor. Blend until everything is well combined.
2. Shape the mixture into equal balls using damp hands; arrange them in the lightly-greased Air Fryer cooking basket.
3. Air fry your falafel at 190°C/375°F for about 20 minutes, shaking the basket halfway through the cooking time.
4. Bon appétit!

Cauliflower Wings

Make these delicious vegan "wings" with simple ingredients you already have in your kitchen. Serve warm cauliflower wings with a hot mayo sauce for dipping.

Preparation Time	Cooking Time	Servings
5 min	**12 min**	**4**

Nutritional Information Per Serving

Energy value: 12 Kcal, Protein: 3.9g,
Carbohydrates: 13.4g, Fats: 4.7g

Ingredients
- 600g cauliflower florets
- 1 tbsp. olive oil
- 1 tbsp. soy sauce
- ½ tsp. cumin, ground
- ½ tsp. onion granules
- ½ tsp. garlic granules
- ½ tsp. red pepper flakes, crushed
- Sea salt and ground black pepper, to taste

Instructions
1. Place the cauliflower florets and the rest of the ingredients in a resealable bag; give it a good shake until the cauliflower florets are well coated on all sides.
2. Air fry the cauliflower florets at 200°C/395°F for 12 minutes, shaking the basket halfway through the cooking time.
3. Bon appétit!

Tofu Nuggets

Ground cumin, garlic, and nutritional yeast give these fried and breaded tofu bites an irresistible flavour! These vegan nuggets go perfectly with chips, tomato-based dipping sauce, and a fresh salad.

Preparation Time	Cooking Time	Servings
5 min	**15 min**	**4**

Nutritional Information Per Serving

Energy value: 334 Kcal, Protein: 17.6g,
Carbohydrates: 41.4g, Fats: 11.2g

Ingredients
- 100g plain flour
- 50ml soy milk
- ½ tsp. baking powder
- ½ tsp. turmeric powder
- 100g breadcrumbs
- 1 tsp. garlic granules
- ½ tsp. ground cumin
- 20g nutritional yeast
- 500g tofu, pressed and cubed
- 1 tbsp. olive oil

Instructions
1. To begin, set up your breading station. Mix the flour with so milk, baking powder, and turmeric powder in a shallow dish. I a separate dish, mix the breadcrumbs, garlic granules, cumir and nutritional yeast.
2. Dip tofu cubes in the flour mixture, pass them onto the so milk, and then press them into the breadcrumb mixture, coatin evenly. Brush the tofu cubes with olive oil.
3. Place the tofu nuggets in the lightly-greased Air Fryer cookin basket. Cook the tofu nuggets at 190°C/375°F for about 1 minutes.
4. Bon appétit!

Easy Granola

With any old-fashioned rolled oat and seeds, this granola is not only tasty but healthy too. Serve with vegan yoghurt and blueberries for an amazing result.

Preparation Time	Cooking Time	Servings
5 min	5 min	5

Nutritional Information Per Serving

Energy value: 287 Kcal, Protein: 9.7g,
Carbohydrates: 25.6g, Fats: 17.6g

Ingredients

- 100g rolled oats
- 50g peanut butter
- 50g pumpkin seeds
- 20g sesame seeds
- 20g hemp seeds
- 40g walnuts, roughly chopped
- 40g agave syrup
- ¼ tsp. ground cloves
- ½ tsp. ground cinnamon

Instructions

Begin by preheating your Air Fryer to 180°C/360°F.
In a mixing bowl, thoroughly combine all the ingredients.
Spoon the granola ingredients into a parchment-lined roasting tin; press down slightly using a silicone spatula.
Bake your granola for approximately 15 minutes. Let it cool before trying it, and store in an air-tight container. Enjoy!

Crispy Paprika Chickpeas

Need an easy, delicious recipe for a vegan snack? Thanks to your Air Fryer, you can roast canned chickpeas in 15 minutes and have more time to enjoy the family night!

Preparation Time	Cooking Time	Servings
5 min	15 min	4

Nutritional Information Per Serving

Energy value: 112 Kcal, Protein: 4.5g,
Carbohydrates: 14g, Fats: 4.7g

Ingredients

- 200g canned chickpeas, drained and rinsed
- 1 tbsp. olive oil
- 1 tsp. smoked paprika
- Sea salt and ground black pepper, to taste

Instructions

1. Toss the drained and rinsed chickpeas with the other ingredients.
2. Place the chickpeas in the Air Fryer cooking basket.
3. Air fry the chickpeas at 200°C/395°F for about 15 minutes, shaking the basket a couple of times.
4. Your snack is ready!

Potato and Kale Croquettes

This is the perfect plant-based, budget-friendly recipe that everyone will love. Serve your croquettes with mayonnaise, Dijon mustard, fresh salad, or dipping sauce of choice.

Preparation Time	Cooking Time	Servings
5 min	45 min	3

Nutritional Information Per Serving

Energy value: 521 Kcal, Protein: 14.2g,
Carbohydrates: 95g, Fats: 9.5g

Ingredients

- 3 medium potatoes, peeled and grated
- 200g kale, chopped
- 1 small onion, finely chopped
- 1 garlic clove, minced
- 1 tbsp. fresh parsley, chopped
- 1 tbsp. milled flaxseed
- 20ml soy milk
- 100g crushed crackers
- Sea salt and ground black pepper, to taste
- 1 tsp. olive oil

Instructions

1. Add the potatoes to a large saucepan of boiling water. Cook until they are fork-tender, for about 30 minutes.
2. Process the potatoes using a potato ricer and combine them with the remaining ingredients. Shape the mixture into small patties and place them in the lightly-greased cooking basket.
3. Bake your fritters at 180°C/360°F for 15 minutes, until thoroughly cooked and crispy on the outside.
4. Bon appétit!

Millet and Bean Burgers

Prepare healthy and light plant-based burgers with soaked millet, canned beans, and spices. The secret ingredient is a good-quality barbecue sauce.

Preparation Time	Cooking Time	Servings
5 min	17 min	4

Nutritional Information Per Serving

Energy value: 312 Kcal, Protein: 10.8g,
Carbohydrates: 56g, Fats: 5.1g

Ingredients

- 200g millet, soaked overnight and rinsed
- 200g canned red kidney beans, drained, and rinsed
- 1 tbsp. tahini
- 1 small onion, finely chopped
- 2 garlic cloves, crushed
- 2 tbsp. vegan BBQ sauce
- Sea salt and ground black pepper, to taste
- 50g breadcrumbs

Instructions

1. In a mixing bowl, thoroughly combine all the ingredients. Shape the mixture into four patties and arrange them in the lightly greased Air Fryer cooking basket.
2. Cook the millet burgers at 180°C/360°F for approximately 1 minutes, until thoroughly cooked and crispy on the outside.
3. Bon appétit!

BBQ Soy Curls

These delicious soy curls are seriously addictive! Serve warm soy curls in a flatbread or burger buns with your favourite toppings.

Preparation Time	Cooking Time	Servings
10 min	13 min	2

Nutritional Information Per Serving

Energy value: 152 Kcal, Protein: 11.6g,
Carbohydrates: 11.6g, Fats: 7.4g

Ingredients

- 50g soy curls
- 50ml hot water
- 2 tbsp. vegan BBQ sauce
- ½ tsp. garlic granules
- ½ tsp. chilli pepper flakes
- 1 tbsp. olive oil

Instructions

Soak the soy curls in hot water for approximately 10 minutes. Drain the soy curls in a mesh sieve, squeezing out all excess liquid.
Toss the soy curls with the remaining ingredients and place them in the lightly-greased cooking basket.
Cook the soy curls at 180°C/360°F for approximately 13 minutes, until thoroughly cooked.
Bon appétit!

Cauliflower Croquettes

Pack extra flavour into your croquettes with carrot and onion. This is a super-quick vegan dish to enjoy with ketchup, mayonnaise, and chips.

Preparation Time	Cooking Time	Servings
5 min	12 min	3

Nutritional Information Per Serving

Energy value: 295 Kcal, Protein: 10.2g,
Carbohydrates: 48.1g, Fats: 7.4g

Ingredients

- 400g cauliflower, grated
- 1 small carrot, grated
- 1 medium onion, finely chopped
- 2 garlic cloves, finely chopped
- 100ml soy milk
- 40g plain flour
- 100g dried breadcrumbs
- 1 tbsp. olive oil

Instructions

1. In a mixing bowl, mix the cauliflower, carrots, onion, garlic, soy milk, and flour and stir until everything is well incorporated.
2. Shape the mixture into small balls and slightly flatten them with a fork. Place the breadcrumbs in a shallow dish.
3. Roll the balls into the breadcrumbs and brush them with olive oil.
4. Transfer them to the lightly oiled Air Fryer cooking basket and bake in the preheated Air Fryer at 190°C/375°F for 6 minutes. Turn them over and cook for a further 6 minutes.
5. Serve immediately and enjoy!

"Cheese" Brussels Sprouts

Upgrade simple roasted Brussels sprouts with vegan staples such as nutritional yeast and tahini. It a brilliant way to add extra protein and vitamins to humble vegetables and serve a complete vegan meal.

Preparation Time	Cooking Time	Servings
10 min	15 min	4

Nutritional Information Per Serving

Energy value: 117 Kcal, Protein: 11.6g,
Carbohydrates: 21.9g, Fats: 5.7g

Ingredients
- 500g Brussels sprouts, trimmed and halved
- 1 tsp. extra-virgin olive oil
- 15ml agave syrup
- 15ml balsamic vinegar
- ½ tsp. garlic granules
- Sea salt and ground black pepper, to taste
- 100g nutritional yeast
- 2 tbsp. tahini

Instructions
1. Toss Brussels sprouts with olive oil, agave syrup, vinegar, garlic granules, salt, and black pepper until they are well coated on all sides.
2. Air fry your Brussels sprouts at 180°C/360°F for 7 to 8 minutes; shake the basket and continue to cook for a further 7 to 8 minutes.
3. Toss Brussels sprouts with nutritional yeast and tahini.
4. Bon appétit!

Spinach Polenta Stacks

An easy recipe for fried polenta with a squidgy middle and crispy surface will impress you! As for topping ideas, let your imagination run wild!

Preparation Time	Cooking Time	Servings
5 min + chilling time	35 min	2

Nutritional Information Per Serving

Energy value: 270 Kcal, Protein: 11.8g,
Carbohydrates: 36.8g, Fats: 10.7g

Ingredients
- 170ml vegetable broth
- 70g quick-cook polenta
- 250g bag spinach
- 2tsp. soy butter
- Sea salt and ground black pepper, to taste
- 4 cherry tomatoes halved
- 40g tofu, crumbled
- 1 tbsp. walnuts, chopped
- 4 black olives, pitted and sliced

Instructions
1. In a large saucepan, bring the vegetable broth to a rapid boil. Immediately reduce the heat to a simmer and gradually stir in the polenta, spinach, butter, salt, and black pepper, whisking continuously to avoid lumps.
2. Let it simmer for approximately 4 minutes, until the polenta has thickened. Pour your polenta into a deep tray and let it cool completely.
3. Once your polenta is chilled, cut it into squares or your favourite shapes, using a sharp oiled knife or a cookie cutter.
4. Air fry polenta squares at 200°C/400°F for about 30 minutes, turning them over once or twice to ensure even cooking.
5. Top each polenta piece with the remaining ingredients and serve. Enjoy!

Vegan Gyro

If you thought you had already made everything in your Air Fryer, think twice! Here is the recipe for a delicious vegan gyro you and your family will love!

Preparation Time
10 min

Cooking Time
13 min

Servings
4

Nutritional Information Per Serving

Energy value: 310 Kcal, Protein: 26.5g,
Carbohydrates: 35.5g, Fats: 7.4g

Ingredients

- 100g soy curls
- 100ml hot water
- ½ tsp. garlic granules
- ½ tsp. chili pepper flakes
- 1 tbsp. olive oil
- 30g vegan mayonnaise
- ½ small cucumber, grated and squeezed
- 1 garlic clove, pressed
- 1 tsp. dried dill
- 4 large pita bread

Instructions

Soak the soy curls in hot water for approximately 10 minutes. Drain the soy curls in a mesh sieve, squeezing out all excess liquid.

Toss the soy curls with spices and olive oil, and place them in the lightly-greased cooking basket.

Cook the soy curls at 180°C/360°F for approximately 13 minutes until crispy.

To make vegan tzatziki: mix the mayonnaise, cucumber, garlic, and dill. Add the air-fried soy curls and vegan tzatziki to a pita bread and serve immediately.

Bon appétit!

Vegan Wraps

Sometimes you need a comfort food that doesn't take too long to make. Kids of all ages will love these colourful vegan wraps!

Preparation Time
10 min

Cooking Time
20 min

Servings
2

Nutritional Information Per Serving

Energy value: 448 Kcal, Protein: 15.6g,
Carbohydrates: 41.6g, Fats: 22.2g

Ingredients

- 100g block tofu
- 2 tbsp. vegan mayonnaise
- Ground black pepper, to taste
- ½ tsp. garlic granules
- Red pepper flakes, crushed
- 2 large tortillas
- 1 small avocado, peeled, pitted, and spiced
- 100g Romaine lettuce
- 1 small tomato, sliced

Instructions

1. Press your tofu: Place the folded paper towels on a working surface (preferably a wooden board). Place the block of tofu on the paper towels. Top the tofu with another layer of paper towels. Press it with a heavy pan or a pot filled with water, and leave for at least 30 minutes.
2. Cut your tofu into 4 slices and toss them with mayonnaise, black pepper, garlic, and red pepper flakes.
3. Cook your tofu in the preheated Air Fryer at 200°C/395°F for 15 minutes until golden.
4. Warm tortillas at 160°C/320°F for about 4 minutes. Assemble the tortilla wraps with tofu, avocado, lettuce, and tomatoes. Cut your tortilla wraps into halves and enjoy!

CHAPTER 7
DESSERTS

**Don't Forget To Download Your Bonus PDF With
The Colored Images**

STEP BY STEP Guide To Access-

1. Open Your Phones (Or Any Device You Want The Book On) Back Camera. The Back Camera Is The One You use as if you are taking a picture of someone.
2. Simply point your Camera at the QR code and 'tap' the QR code with your finger to focus the camera.
3. A link / pop up will appear. Simply tap that (and make sure you have internet connection) and the FREE PDF containing all of the colored images should appear.
4. If You Click On The File And It Says 'The File Is Too Big To Preview' Simply click 'Download' and it will download the full book onto your phone!
5. Now you have access to these FOREVER. Simply 'Bookmark' The tab it opened on, or download the document and take wherever you want.
6. Repeat this on any device you want it on!

Any Issues / Feedback/ Troubleshooting please email: anthonypublishing123@gmail.com and our customer service team will help you! We want to make sure you have the BEST experience with our books!

Chocolate Chip Cookies

How about chocolate chip cookies in an Air Fryer? Yes, please! Make plenty, as they're sure to be a hit!

Preparation Time	Cooking Time	Servings
10 min	15 min	5

Nutritional Information Per Serving

Energy value: 375 Kcal, Protein: 4.6g,
Carbohydrates: 40.8g, Fats: 22g

Ingredients

- 75g butter at room temperature
- 80g granulated sugar
- 1 tsp. vanilla extract
- 1 small egg
- 100g plain flour
- ½ tsp. bicarbonate of soda
- A pinch of sea salt
- A pinch of grated nutmeg
- ½ tsp. ground cinnamon
- 100g dark chocolate chips

Instructions

In a mixing bowl, beat the butter, sugar, and vanilla into a cream. Beat in the egg until smooth and creamy.

Sift the flour, bicarbonate of soda, and salt into the mixing bowl and combine well.

Lastly, fold in the chocolate chips and give the dough a gentle stir.

Preheat your Air Fryer to 175°C/350°F. Create small scoops of the batter with a teaspoon, and arrange them on a baking tray. Bake your cookies in the preheated Air Fryer for 15 minutes. Let them rest on a cooling rack for about 10 minutes. Serve and enjoy!

Easy Mince Pies

No rolling – no hassle! This recipe is easy to make in the Air Fryer. Just make sure to find good-quality mincemeat.

Preparation Time	Cooking Time	Servings
10 min	20 min	5

Nutritional Information Per Serving

Energy value: 495 Kcal, Protein: 7g,
Carbohydrates: 70.6g, Fats: 22.6g

Ingredients

- 120g butter, cold and cut into chunks
- 175g plain flour
- 50g brown sugar
- A pinch of salt
- ¼ tsp. vanilla extract
- 100g mincemeat
- 30g prunes, pitted and chopped
- 20g flaked almonds
- 1 small egg, beaten
- Icing sugar to dust

Instructions

1. Rub the butter into the flour until combined; stir in the sugar, salt, and vanilla.
2. Knead the pastry to create a ball (it should look like a shortbread dough). Spray tartlet moulds with non-stick cooking oil. Press small balls of pastry into tartlet moulds using 2/3 of the dough. Use the remaining 1/3 of the dough to create lids.
3. Add mincemeat, prunes, and almonds to your pies and cover them with the lids. Brush them with the beaten egg using a silicone pastry brush.
4. Bake mince pies at 180°C/360°F for about 20 minutes, working with batches if needed. Dust your mince pies with icing sugar just before serving and enjoy!
5.

Anise Bread Pudding Cups

Looking for an easy pudding recipe? Get ready for this amazing Air Fryer recipe that will become a big hit with your family! Dig in!

Preparation Time	Cooking Time	Servings
10 min	20 min	5

Nutritional Information Per Serving
Energy value: 495 Kcal, Protein: 7g,
Carbohydrates: 70.6g, Fats: 22.6g

Ingredients
- 7 thin bread slices, cubed
- 1 small egg, beaten
- 50g brown sugar
- 100g double cream
- 150ml milk
- 1 tsp. ground anise star
- ½ tsp. vanilla extract
- ¼ tsp. ground cinnamon
- A pinch of sea salt
- 50g walnuts, chopped

Instructions
1. Place all the ingredients in a mixing bowl; gently stir with a spatula and set it aside for about 30 minutes.
2. Spoon the mixture into lightly-greased muffin cases.
3. Bake the bread pudding cups at 180°C/360°F for about 20 minutes until golden-brown.
4. Bon appétit!

Chocolate Brownies

To melt the chocolate chunks, you can add the chocolate along with butter in a heatproof bowl, and set it over a pan of simmering water. Whisk the mixture continuously until it has fully melted.

Preparation Time	Cooking Time	Servings
15 min	20 min	5

Nutritional Information Per Serving
Energy value: 344 Kcal, Protein: 5.5g,
Carbohydrates: 39.4g, Fats: 18.2g

Ingredients
- 70g unsalted butter, room temperature
- 100g dark chocolate (70-85% cacao solids), cut into chunks
- 100g brown sugar
- 2 small eggs, lightly beaten
- 50g plain flour
- 20g oat flour
- ¼ tsp. ground cinnamon
- ¼ tsp. ground cloves
- 1 tsp. pure vanilla paste

Instructions
1. Begin by preheating your Air Fryer to 175°C/350°F. Butter baking tin and set it aside.
2. Melt the chocolate along with the butter and sugar at 120°C/250°F for about 2 minutes. Keep a close eye on it.
3. Next, fold in the egg and beat again to combine well. Stir in the other ingredients and mix until everything is well combined.
4. Bake your brownies in the preheated Air Fryer for 20 to 2 minutes. Let them rest on a cooling rack for about 15 minute before slicing and serving.
5. Bon appétit!

Stuffed Apples

An old-fashioned, healthy dessert you can make in no time! Pecans, fresh ginger root, and candied orange peel bring a deep, oriental flavour, while raisins bring those homey, cosy elements to baked apples. They are absolutely delicious!

Preparation Time	Cooking Time	Servings
5 min	18 min	3

Nutritional Information Per Serving

Energy value: 333 Kcal, Protein: 55.6g,
Carbohydrates: 33.6g Fats: 12.3g

Ingredients

- 3 medium apples
- 50g quick-cooking oats
- 50g pecan, roughly chopped
- 30g raisins
- 30g honey
- 1 tsp. fresh ginger, peeled and grated
- 1tbsp. candied orange peel
- ½ teaspoon cinnamon powder

Instructions

1. Remove the stems and seeds from the apples and use a spoon to scoop out the flesh from the middle.
2. In a mixing bowl, thoroughly combine the remaining ingredients. Spoon the filling mixture into the prepared apples.
3. Lower the apples into the lightly-greased Air Fryer cooking basket and bake at 170°C/340°F for 18 minutes.
4. Serve at room temperature and enjoy!

Chocolate and Blackberry Wontons

These berry chocolatey wontons are sure to be your new favourite Sunday dessert. Kids will love these super-cute bites!

Preparation Time	Cooking Time	Servings
5 min	12 min	4

Nutritional Information Per Serving

Energy value: 401 Kcal, Protein: 9.9g,
Carbohydrates: 60.9g, Fats: 12.7g

Ingredients

- 100g chocolate chips
- 100g blackberries, mashed
- 8 (10 cm) wonton wrappers
- 1 egg, lightly whisked with 1 tablespoon of water (egg wash)
- 40g chocolate syrup

Instructions

1. Divide the chocolate chips and blackberries among wonton wrappers. Next, fold the wrappers diagonally in half over the filling; press the edges together with a fork and brush the wontons with the egg wash.
2. Bake your wontons at 185°C/370°F for 12 minutes, until they are hot and golden.
3. Decorate the sweet wontons with chocolate syrup and enjoy!

Mug Cake

If you need a quick single-serving dessert, try making this simple Air Fryer mug cake with easy ingredients you already have at home. Serve with a scoop of vanilla ice cream.

Preparation Time	Cooking Time	Servings
5 min	11 min	1

Nutritional Information Per Serving

Energy value: 401 Kcal, Protein: 9.9g,
Carbohydrates: 60.9g, Fats: 12.7g

Ingredients

- 50g milk chocolate chunks
- 1 tsp. coconut oil
- 1 tsp. double cream
- 2 teaspoons self-raising flour

Instructions

1. Spoon the chocolate chunks, coconut oil, and double cream into a lightly-greased ramekin.
2. Melt the mixture at 120°C/250°F for 2 minutes.
3. Stir in the flour. Bake your mug cake at 180°C/360°F for about 9 minutes. Devour!

Roasted Fruit Salad

This is a great way to get kids to eat more fruit! You can use any fruit you have on hand, as long as they have similar cooking times in the Air Fryer.

Preparation Time	Cooking Time	Servings
5 min	11 min	2

Nutritional Information Per Serving

Energy value: 140 Kcal, Protein: 0.9g,
Carbohydrates: 24.9g, Fats: 4.7g

Ingredients

- 100g fresh pineapple, cut into bite-sized pieces
- 100g apple, cored and diced
- 1 tbsp. fresh lemon juice
- 1 tbsp. honey
- 1 tbsp. coconut, shredded
- ½ tsp. vanilla paste
- ¼ tsp. cinnamon powder

Instructions

1. Toss all ingredients in a mixing bowl. Let them stand for about 15 minutes to absorb the flavours and release the juices.
2. Air fry your fruits at 190°C/390°F for 10 minutes, until tender and caramelized. Make sure to give it a good shake halfway through the cooking time.
3. Enjoy!

Banana Muffins

These appetizing banana muffins make a delicious and easy dessert. You can replace butter with peanut butter to add more flavour to your muffins.

 Preparation Time 10 min

 Cooking Time 20 min

 Servings 6

Nutritional Information Per Serving

Energy value: 26 Kcal, Protein: 4.6g,
Carbohydrates: 35.1g, Fats: 5.5g

Ingredients

1 egg, beaten
130g self-raising flour
1 tsp. bicarbonate of soda
50g light brown muscovado sugar
2 small bananas, mashed
60ml buttermilk
30g melted butter
½ tsp. vanilla paste
½ tsp. ground cinnamon
2 tbsp. old-fashioned rolled oats

Instructions

Start by preheating your Air Fryer to 175°C/350°F. Brush a muffin tin (with 6 muffin cases) with non-stick cooking oil.
In a large mixing bowl, beat the egg until pale and frothy; gradually and carefully pour in the other liquid ingredients. Stir in the dry ingredients slowly in the order listed above. Use a wire whisk until a smooth batter forms, but do not overmix your batter.
Spoon the batter into the prepared muffin tin. Cook the muffins for approximately 20 minutes. Leave them to cool completely before unmoulding and serving.
Bon appétit!

Peanut Butter Cinnamon Cookies

This is hands-down the easiest cookie recipe ever! You can use both crunchy and smooth peanut butter for the recipe.

 Preparation Time 10 min

Cooking Time 12 min

 Servings 4

Nutritional Information Per Serving

Energy value: 161 Kcal, Protein: 2.8g,
Carbohydrates: 26.2g, Fats: 4.9g

Ingredients

- 100g peanut butter
- 1 tsp. cinnamon powder
- ½ tsp. pure vanilla extract
- 80g golden caster sugar
- A pinch of flaky sea salt
- 1 small egg

Instructions

1. Begin by preheating your Air Fryer to 175°C/350°F.
2. In a mixing bowl, beat the peanut butter, cinnamon, vanilla, and sugar until creamy and uniform. Next, fold in the egg and beat again until the mixture forms a dough.
3. Create small scoops of the dough and place them, well-spaced apart, on a cookie tin.
4. Bake your cookies in the preheated Air Fryer for 12 minutes, until golden around the edges.
5. Serve and enjoy!

Chocolate Cupcakes

Try these healthy chocolate cupcakes with quinoa and banana. Serve them with dollops of ice cream and enjoy!

Preparation Time	Cooking Time	Servings
15 min	22 min	6

Nutritional Information Per Serving
Energy value: 283 Kcal, Protein: 2.6g,
Carbohydrates: 37.6g, Fats: 13g

Ingredients
- 100g dark chocolate (70-85% cacao solids), cut into chunks
- 70g unsalted butter, room temperature
- 100g golden caster sugar
- 2 tbsp. honey
- 1 small banana, peeled and mashed
- 100g quinoa, cooked drained rinsed
- ¼ tsp. ground cinnamon
- 1 tsp. vanilla paste

Instructions
1. Begin by preheating your Air Fryer to 175°C/350°F. Butter a baking tin and set it aside.
2. Melt the chocolate along with the butter and sugar at 120°C/250°F for about 2 minutes. Keep a close eye on it.
3. Next, fold in the honey, mashed banana, and quinoa, and beat again to combine well. Stir in the cinnamon and vanilla, and mix until everything is well combined.
4. Bake your brownies in the preheated Air Fryer for 20 to 22 minutes. Let them rest on a cooling rack for about 15 minutes before slicing and serving.
5. Bon appétit!

Mini Berry Cheesecakes

With their silky topping and golden crust, you'd hardly guess these elegant cheesecakes are cooked in an Air Fryer – It takes only 15 minutes to cook and doesn't require too much effort.

Preparation Time	Cooking Time	Servings
10 min + chilling time	15 min	4

Nutritional Information Per Serving
Energy value: 414 Kcal, Protein: 10.2g,
Carbohydrates: 38.6g, Fats: 24.3g

Ingredients
- 50g powdered sugar
- 120g plain flour
- 75g butter, unsalted, room temperature
- 150g mascarpone cheese, room temperature
- 1 tsp. vanilla paste
- 100g fresh or frozen mixed berries

Instructions
1. Beat the sugar with flour and butter until well combined. Press the mixture into the bottom of lightly-greased ramekins.
2. Bake them at 175°C/350°F for about 15 minutes. Then, transfer the ramekins to the freezer and let them sit for about 30 minutes.
3. Next, make the cheesecake topping by mixing the cheese, vanilla, and 50 grams of mixed berries. Place this topping over the crust and transfer your cheesecake in the freezer for further 30 minutes.
4. Garnish with the remaining berries and serve well chilled.
5. Bon appétit!

Apple Fritters

Use a simple batter with a few easy-to-find ingredients to make this old-fashion dessert. Traditionally, apple fritters are made by dropping battered apple slices into the hot oil. This is a great way to get an apple fritter taste without all that grease.

Preparation Time	Cooking Time	Servings
5 min	13 min	4

Nutritional Information Per Serving

Energy value: 255 Kcal, Protein: 5.6g,
Carbohydrates: 51.3g, Fats: 3.3g

Ingredients

- 1 large apple, peeled
- 150g cake flour
- 50g granulated sugar
- A pinch of sea salt
- ½ tsp. baking powder
- ½ tsp. cinnamon powder
- 1 medium egg, beaten
- 120 ml cup full-fat milk
- 1 tsp. coconut oil

Instructions

Core the apples and slice them into rings. Mix the flour, sugar, salt, baking powder, and cinnamon. In a separate bowl, whisk the egg with milk; add the wet mixture to the dry ingredients and stir to combine well.

Dip apple rings into the batter and arrange them in the lightly-greased Air Fryer cooking basket.

Cook the apple fritters in the preheated Air Fryer at 185°C/370°F for about 13 minutes, turning them over halfway through the cooking time.

Serve the apple fritters with powdered sugar.

Bon appétit!

Plum Crumble

With fresh plums, rolled oats, and dark rum, this fruity dessert is deliciously fluffy and light. It can be an indulgent end to a family meal or accompany a romantic dinner for two.

Preparation Time	Cooking Time	Servings
10 min	35 min	5

Nutritional Information Per Serving

Energy value: 405 Kcal, Protein: 5.6g,
Carbohydrates: 42.4g, Fats: 26.3g

Ingredients

- 200g plums, pitted and halved
- 1 small lemon, zested
- 1 tbsp. arrowroot powder
- 50g brown sugar

Topping:
- 100g old-fashioned rolled oats
- 50g brown sugar
- 50g coconut oil, melted
- 50 ml dark rum
- ½ tsp. ground cinnamon
- 100g pecans, chopped

Instructions

1. Toss your plums with the zested lemon, arrowroot powder, and sugar. Arrange the plums in a lightly greased baking tray.
2. In a mixing dish, thoroughly combine all the topping ingredients. Sprinkle the topping ingredients over the fruit layer. Place the baking tray in the Air Fryer cooking basket.
3. Bake your crumble in the preheated Air Fryer at 165°C/330°F for about 35 minutes. Let it cool for 10 minutes before serving.
4. Bon appétit!

Authentic Churros

Air-fried to golden perfection, this popular street food is sure to please. Serve with cinnamon sugar or chocolate dipping sauce.

Preparation Time	Cooking Time	Servings
10 min	15 min	5

Nutritional Information Per Serving
Energy value: 348 Kcal, Protein: 3.9g,
Carbohydrates: 35.4g, Fats: 21.6g

Ingredients
- 370g apple juice unsweetened
- 120g butter
- 40g sugar
- ½ tsp. cinnamon powder
- ½ tsp. ground cardamom
- ¼ tsp, ground cloves
- 120g plain flour
- 2 large eggs, beaten

Instructions
1. In a medium saucepan, bring the apple juice, butter, sugar, and spices to a simmer. Let it simmer uncovered, until the butter has fully melted and then turn the heat off.
2. To make the choux pastry, tip in the flour and whisk vigorously to combine well. Return the mixture to the heat and let it simmer again until a smooth ball forms.
3. Then, add the eggs, one at a time, and continue mixing using an electric mixer. The choux pastry should be thick and slightly sticky.
4. Add the choux pastry to a piping bag fitted with an open star tip. Pipe your churros onto the lightly-greased Air Fryer cooking basket and repeat the process with the rest of the choux pastry. Brush the pastry with non-stick oil.
5. Air fry your churros at 190°C/375°F for approximately 12 minutes, until golden brown. Work in batches, if needed. Enjoy!

Banana Fritters

If you are looking for an easy, delectable dessert, make banana fritters in your Air Fryer. The secret to the best fritters is to use very ripe bananas.

Preparation Time	Cooking Time	Servings
10 min	12 min	4

Nutritional Information Per Serving
Energy value: 155 Kcal, Protein: 3.3g,
Carbohydrates: 24.8g, Fats: 5.2g

Ingredients
- 50g self-raising flour
- ½ tsp. bicarbonate of soda
- A pinch of sea salt
- A pinch of grated nutmeg
- 1 small egg
- 2 tbsp. golden caster sugar
- 30ml full-fat coconut milk
- 2 medium ripe bananas, peeled and mashed
- 1 tsp. non-stick oil

Instructions
1. In a mixing bowl, thoroughly combine the flour, bicarbonate of soda, salt, and nutmeg.
2. Carefully separate the egg yolk from the egg white. Beat the egg yolk with sugar and milk until pale and frothy. Then, beat the egg white until stiff peaks form.
3. Gradually and carefully, add the egg white to the mixture.
4. Add the liquid mixture to the dry ingredients; fold in the mashed banana and mix to combine well.
5. Add a parchment paper liner inside the cooking basket. Use a cookie scoop to create the dollops of batter, brush with your oil of choice, and air fry the banana fritters at 185°C/365°F for approximately 8 minutes until golden brown. Enjoy!

Crème Brûlée

Five ingredients and 30 minutes are all you'll need to make a restaurant-style crème brûlée. The secret ingredient is a vanilla bean paste.

Preparation Time

10 min

Cooking Time
27 min

Servings
4

Nutritional Information Per Serving
Energy value: 155 Kcal, Protein: 3.3g, Carbohydrates: 24.8g, Fats: 5.2g

Ingredients

- 4 egg yolks
- ½ tsp. vanilla bean paste
- 100g golden caster sugar
- 400 ml double cream
- 4 tbsp. brown sugar

Instructions

Beat the egg yolks, vanilla, sugar, and cream in a saucepan over low heat. Let it cook until the sugar has dissolved. Pour the mixture into four ramekins.

Preheat your Air Fryer to 190°C/380°F and air-fry the crème brûlée for about 25 minutes.

Sprinkle brown sugar over the top of each ramekin and caramelize the top at 200°C/395°F for about 2 minutes.

Bon appétit!

Pear Pie Samosas

Discover how to make the ultimate pie samosas in your Air Fryer! You can double or triple the recipe and enjoy these hand pies at the next dinner party with family and friends!

Preparation Time

10 min

Cooking Time
13 min

Servings
4

Nutritional Information Per Serving
Energy value: 335 Kcal, Protein: 3.7g, Carbohydrates: 56.3g, Fats: 11.5g

Ingredients

- 4 sheets filo pastry
- 2 medium pears, peeled, cored, and chopped
- 60g caster sugar
- 60g raisins

Instructions

1. Cut the sheets of filo pastry in thirds lengthways. Divide the filling between pastry strips; fold over to form triangular parcels and repeat.
2. Brush your samosas with non-stick oil and cook them at 175°C/350°F for 13 minutes or until slightly brown.
3. Dust with powdered sugar and enjoy!

Berry Crisp

Using rolled oats, melted butter, almonds, and pure vanilla paste is the perfect way to achieve a great, crispy coating for your favourite Air Fryer dessert. You can also use mixed berries or blueberries for this recipe.

Preparation Time	Cooking Time	Servings
10 min	35 min	6

Nutritional Information Per Serving
Energy value: 385 Kcal, Protein: 6.9g,
Carbohydrates: 40.4g, Fats: 23.3g

Ingredients
- 200g blackberries
- 1 tsp. fresh ginger, peeled and grated
- 1 tbsp. corn starch
- 50g brown sugar

Topping:
- 100g old-fashioned rolled oats
- 100g butter, melted
- 2 tbsp. pure maple syrup
- 50g brown sugar
- 1 tsp. vanilla paste
- ½ tsp. ground cinnamon
- 100g almonds, chopped

Instructions
1. Toss your blackberries with ginger, corn starch, and sugar. Arrange the blackberries in a lightly-greased souffle dish.
2. In a mixing dish, place the oats, butter, maple syrup, sugar, vanilla, cinnamon, and almonds. Mix until the topping mixture comes together in loose clumps. Pour the mixture over the fruit layer.
3. Place the baking tray in the Air Fryer cooking basket and bake the berry crisp in the preheated Air Fryer at 165°C/330°F for about 35 minutes.
4. Bon appétit!

Chocolate Fudge with Almonds

Make this gooey fudge in your Air Fryer and impress your guests at the next dinner party! This foolproof traditional recipe is ready in less than 30 minutes.

Preparation Time	Cooking Time	Servings
10 min	20 min	6

Nutritional Information Per Serving
Energy value: 452 Kcal, Protein: 9.5g,
Carbohydrates: 41.4g, Fats: 28.2g

Ingredients
Cake:
- 70g unsalted butter, room temperature
- 100g dark chocolate (70-85% cacao solids), cut into chunks
- 20g cocoa powder
- 1 small egg
- 100g brown sugar
- 30 oat flour
- ¼ tsp. ground cinnamon
- 30g almonds, chopped

Topping:
- 130ml tin condensed milk
- 80g smooth peanut butter
- 100g dark chocolate (70-85% cacao solids), cut into chunks

Instructions
1. Begin by preheating your Air Fryer to 175°C/350°F. Butter baking tin and set it aside.
2. Set an ovenproof bowl over a pan of simmering water and ad the butter, chocolate, and cocoa powder to the bowl. Whisk th mixture until it has fully melted.
3. In a mixing dish, beat the egg with sugar until frothy; add the oa flour, cinnamon, and almonds, and mix to combine. Fold in th chocolate mixture and stir until everything is well incorporate
4. Bake your brownies in the preheated Air Fryer for 20 to 2 minutes, until a wooden tester in the middle comes out wi sticky crumbs.
5. Meanwhile, set an ovenproof bowl over a pan of simmerin water. Add the topping ingredients to the bowl and whisk un it has fully melted.
6. Afterwards, spread the topping mixture over the cooled fudg base. Let it rest on a cooling rack for about 10 minutes befo serving. Enjoy!

Apple Chips

For the best results, do not overcrowd the cooking basket and work in batches. Keep your apple chips in an airtight container for up to 5 days.

Preparation Time	Cooking Time	Servings
10 min	10 min	2

Nutritional Information Per Serving

Energy value: 52 Kcal, Protein: 0.3g,
Carbohydrates: 13.4g, Fats: 0.2g

Ingredients

1 medium apple
1 tsp. cinnamon powder

Instructions

Cut your apple into ½ cm-thick slices, using a sharp knife or mandolin.
Air fry apple chips at 190°C/380°F for approximately 10 minutes.
Toss the apple chips in the cinnamon powder.
Allow the apple chips to sit for about 10 minutes before serving and storing.
Bon appétit!

Printed in Great Britain
by Amazon

17777669R00056